Guide to the
Birds of Iceland

Þorsteinn Einarsson

Guide to the Birds of Iceland

English translation and revision of bird descriptions:
Jóhann Óli Hilmarsson with the assistance of Ólafur Karl Nielsen.

When the book was first published in Icelandic in 1987 Kristinn Haukur
Skarphéðinsson read the text and gave advice on photos and drawings.

ÖRN OG ÖRLYGUR PUBLISHING HOUSE 1991

ISBN 9979-55-007-4

GUIDE TO THE BIRDS OF ICELAND

Text: © Copyright 1991: Örn og Örlygur Publishing House
Photographs: © Copyright see list page 229
Design: Sigurþór Jakobsson
Drawings: Sigurður Valur Sigurðsson
Map, chart and drawing of bird-cliff, based on the author's sketches: Valur Skarphéðinsson
Typesetting: G. Ben. prentstofa hf.
Colour separations and filmwork: Prentmyndastofan hf. and Prentþjónustan hf.
Printing and binding: G. Ben. prentstofa hf.

Contents

Foreword

The Reykjavík publishing house *Örn og Örlygur* has devoted a major part of its output to reference books about Iceland, its natural environment, culture and ethnology. These publications have always been distinguished by high standards in text, illustrations and overall production.

Travel guides and handbooks have formed one group of these books from *Örn og Örlygur*. Among them is the present *Guide to the Birds of Iceland*, which was first published in Icelandic as *Fuglahandbókin* in 1987.

The guide was the first practical guide to identification of bird species to appear in Iceland. The Icelandic edition proved to be highly popular and the print run was sold out in three years.

Guide to the Birds of Iceland was written by Þorsteinn Einarsson (b. 1911), a teacher who began studying and observing birds 55 years ago, Jóhann Óli Hilmarsson (b. 1954), who has been involved in watching, studying and photographing birds for 20 years, and Kristinn Haukur Skarphéðinsson (b. 1956), who has been watching birds for 20 years and is now studying for the degree of Ph.D. in Ornithology at the University of Wisconsin, U.S.A.

Credits for photographs and drawings appear on p. 227.

The text was translated by Jóhann Óli Hilmarsson, together with Dr. Ólafur Karl Nielsen, a graduate of Cornell University, who now works on research in Ornithology. Jón Skaptason, Ph.D., reviewed the translation and read the proofs. The introductory notes on the use of the book and the general texts at the beginning of each section were translated by Jeffrey Cosser, who also looked over the proofs.

Iceland lies at the boundary of two zoogeographical zones, the Nearctic and the Palaearctic. Throughout the year, the bird life of the country reflects the rhythms in the life-cycles of the birds of these regions, and is interesting from the point of view of species and their interbreeding. Few areas in the world of similar size contain as great a variety and combination of bird habitats as Iceland: mountainous country with areas of vegetation extending up to the glaciers; wetlands with tundra vegetation and sand dunes; moorland crossed by valleys and heather-covered heaths; sand-flats with bare rocks and cliffs; stony soil with sparse vegetation; valleys leading off fjords and bordered by steep cliffs with scree at their base; moorland covered with hummocks; scrub and forest; lava fields with and without vegetation; mudflats and river deltas; coastal sand dunes covered with lyme-grass; lakes with islets both in the lowlands and the highlands; sand beaches, pebble beaches and erosion banks; offshore islands; nesting cliffs (some 10 km in length and up to 500 m high, homes to thousands of birds); farmland, forestry plantations and domestic gardens.

It is my hope that visitors to Iceland will use this guide in their travels through these varied habitats, enjoy them to the full and derive the added pleasure from the birds they see. Finally I should like to thank the publishers for their initiative in bringing the book out in English, and all those who contributed to the production of this edition and in particular Hálfdan Ómar Hálfdanarson for overseeing the project. It is my hope that their efforts will prove to have been worth while.

Summer 1991,
Þorsteinn Einarsson.

A Note on the Photographs

The photographs in this guide were chosen with the aim of showing the main characteristics of each species as clearly as possible. With this principle in mind, we often had to reject good photographs which did not show the features essential for identification, while on the other hand we sometimes chose photographs which did not meet the strictest demands regarding focus or grain. We tried to choose photos which had not previously been published in this country, but this proved difficult in some cases.

Only a handful of Icelanders are involved in serious bird photography. They all contributed material to this guide, with the exception of one who was unable to do so for the good reason that his own book had been published shortly before this guide first appeared. Assistance was also sought from various other people who were known or believed to have taken some photographs of birds, though there was not time to explore all such channels. Nearly all those approached were willing to allow their photographs to be published. When it became clear that we could not always find Icelandic photographs, we looked further afield, as birds are by nature not limited to any one country and are not bound by national boundaries in their migrations round the globe. Hans van Brandwijk, of the Netherlands, a photographer who has pursued the subject in Iceland, amongst other places, kindly granted permission to use some of his photographs, and Marianne Vibholm at Biofoto in Copenhagen obliged by permitting the use of that company's extensive and excellent photo library.

I made the initial selection from the photographs we received, and the final choice was made after examination by the author, Þorsteinn Einarsson, the publisher, Örlygur Hálfdanarson, the designers, Valur Skarphéðinsson and Sigurþór Jakobsson, and also Kristinn Haukur Skarphéðinsson and others.

The guide contains about 170 photographs, all of which are printed from slides.

Finally, I should like to thank all the photographers, everyone else who played a part in choosing the photographs, as I have mentioned above, and all the others involved in the project, for their pleasant and informative co-operation.

Jóhann Óli Hilmarsson

●Grímsey

Hraunhafnartangi

Raufarhöfn● ●
●Melrakka-
slétta
ÞISTIL-
FJÖRÐUR
ÖXAR-
FJÖRÐUR ●Kópasker
Langanes

●Þórshöfn

BAKKAFLÓI

Flatey
SKJÁLF-Tjörnes
ANDI ● HÚSAVÍK
Ásbyrgi

●Bakkafjörður

EYJA
R
Húsey
Grenivík

Laxá

Dettifoss

Vopnafjörður

HÉRAÐS-
FLÓI

Austfirðir
(East Fjords)

KUR
UREYRI

Goða-
foss

Krafla
Reykjahlíð
1

Jökulsá á Fjöllum

Grímsstaðir

Mývatn

Möðrudalur

Smjörfjöll

Bakkagerði ●

Jagartjörn

1

SEYÐISFJÖRÐUR

EGILSSTAÐIR ● Dalatangi

Mývatnsöræfi

ÓDÁÐAHRAUN
Herðubreið

Hallormsstaður

NESKAUPSTAÐUR ●

ESKIFJÖRÐUR ●

Gerpir

Askja

Reyðarfjörður●
1

Búðir●

Vesturöræfi

SPRENGISANDUR

Trölladyngja

Snæfell

Stöðvarfjörður●
Breiðdalsvík●

KULL

Tungnafells-
jökull
Nýidalur
árver
Bárðarbunga
Kverkfjöll

●Djúpivogur
Papey

1

VATNAJÖKULL

Grímsvötn

Hornafjörður
HÖFN

ívötn
Lakagígar

ÖRÆFA-
Skaftafell Hvannadalshnjúkur
JÖKULL
Lóma-
gnúpur

Skeiðarársandur
Fagurhólsmýri

●Kirkjubæjarklaustur
Ingólfshöfði

Hjörleifshöfði

Útgáfu og höfundarréttur eign Landmælinga Íslands.

Eftirgerð bönnuð. Copyright © 1991

Kortagerð: Ólafur Valsson

9

Notes on Icelandic Birds and the Use of this Book

By following the instructions in words and pictures below, it should be possible to identify 110 species of birds. Of this number, 70 species are regular breeders in Iceland, i.e. they lay eggs and rear young in this country. The other 40 species discussed in the book are regular passage visitors (8), regular annual visitors (3), winter visitors (6), summer visitors (1) and vagrants (23). Some of these species (at least 15) have tried breeding in Iceland.

Eighteen breeding species live in Iceland all year round, i.e. are residents, 9 are residents for most of the year (resident/migrants), and 16 species live in Iceland less than half of the year, as most of their stocks are migrants (migrant/residents). According to this classification, 43 breeding species may be seen in Iceland during the winter. To this number must be added the six regular winter visitors and a variable number of vagrant species. Annual counts taken at the winter equinox have shown that in the south-west of the country the number of species can be well over 70, and in 31 years a total of 99 species have been recorded.

In the spring, in addition to the 43 breeding species which are to be seen here all year round there are the 27 migrant species which come to breed and stay for the summer, one summer visitor species, eight passage visitors and some of the frequent vagrants (23), making a total of about 90 species which can be seen in the country in early summer. All in all, it is estimated that over 300 species of birds have been sighted in Iceland.

Of the 110 species described in the book, the sexes of 32 species are differentiated and 24 species change their plumage in the winter. To add to the variety, there are certain other annual changes in plumage and separate plumages for immature birds, which in some cases undergo constant changes for 3–4 years before assuming the final colouring of the adult birds. For the inexperienced observer, these variations appear to add even further to the variety of species.

This book is intended to answer the question which occurs frequently to anyone who travels through Iceland in any season of the year: "What sort of bird is that?"

The descriptions fall into eight sections: 1. Seabirds; 2. Waders; 3. Gulls, Terns and Skuas; 4. Pigeons and Doves; 5. Waterfowl; 6. Gallinaceous Birds; 7. Birds of Prey and Owls and 8. Passerines.

Above the description of each bird, the heading contains the species name in English and Latin. Larger type is used for those species which breed and rear young regularly in Iceland than for those which either do not nest regularly or raise young in the country. Important information is recorded underneath the lower line enclosing the heading: the length in centimetres, whether the species is a breeder, passage migrant, summer or winter visitor or a vagrant, and whether the male is identical to, similar to or different from the female. The last number indicates the size group of the bird in question.

Seven size groups of birds are mentioned in the Introduction (pp 12–13). A typical reference species is given for each size group, namely: 1. Snow Bunting; 2. Redwing; 3. Golden Plover; 4. Whimbrel; 5. Mallard; 6. Raven; 7. Great Black-backed Gull.

The first thing for the observer to decide when identifying a bird is which group it belongs to. If the sighting is made in the summer, the habitat frequently gives the best hint on what section to consult in the book. During the winter the environment is not as informative, as the birds' habitat selection is narrower and restricted largely to the sea, the intertidal zone, harbours, human settlements and fish-processing plants. Various hints designed to help the novice birdwatcher are given in the introduction and should be consulted carefully.

If the observer has reached the general conclusion that he is dealing with a sea-bird, he should examine the pictures and read the appropriate descriptions. Now the observer must ask himself how big the bird is, i.e. is it the size of a Raven (class 6)? — No, smaller. The size of a Golden Plover (class 3)? — No, bigger. Similar to a Whimbrel (class 4)? — A little bit bigger. Then it is class 5, including birds the size of a Mallard. Among sea-birds, only the Fulmar and the Sooty Shearwater belong to this size class. If the bird is sighted from a boat off the south coast of Iceland during summer, it could very well be a Sooty Shearwater. These two species have similar flight patterns but their plumage is quite different, the Fulmar being all light and the Sooty Shearwater all dark. If the observer eliminates these two species he must next turn to class 4 among the sea-birds. Five species of seabirds belong to this class. Now it is time to study carefully the small photographs at the side of the text emphasizing the main identification characteristics with numbered arrows. These condensed details should then be compared with the main descriptions and photographs of the birds.

In order for the reader to derive full benefit from reading the text, it is necessary for him to be familiar with the names of the parts of birds and of the various parts of the plumage, e.g. nail, speculum, rump, etc.

By observing closely and using methods of elimination in comparing the image of the bird observed with the photographs and descriptions in the book, or by simultaneous comparison where possible, success should be assured. The main thing is not to be hasty or to indulge in wishful thinking: the facts must be examined and tested, e.g. the size of the bird; its appearance in flight, standing, perching or swimming; the colour and shape of the beak, feet and tail; the colouring of the wings, stripes on the crown, superciliary stripes or eye-stripes; patches on the ear-coverts or the flanks; speckles on the back or breast, etc. In this way, the observer can train himself to look for features which make identification possible. The pre-condition for doing so is a reasonable knowledge of the physical structure of birds (see the diagram on pp. 22–23 and the introduction, pp. 12–21). Bird-watching becomes an even more interesting hobby if people develop the habit of accuracy in all observations of birds' appearance and behaviour. Familiarity developed in this way acts as a spur to further knowledge, which can be gained both through bird-watching and by reading books and articles (see the bibliography on p. 224). Anyone who gives himself up to the pleasures of bird-watching soon becomes deeply involved and reaps unnumbered hours of pleasure as a reward. This book is intended to add to those hours.

What Sort of Bird is That?

This section contains numbered diagrams and drawings which are referred to in the text. The first seven birds are in approximately the correct relative size proportions, but this does not apply to the later drawings, which are intended solely to illustrate points made in the text.

People ask themselves or each other the question "What sort of bird is that?" if they see a bird they don't know. If the answer isn't forthcoming but the observer is really interested to know it, the way to go about it is to fix the image of the bird in one's memory, and then to consult a bird book, if one is to hand, looking up the pictures which resemble the bird that has been seen. If no book is immediately available, the observation must be recorded until one can be found. Under these circumstances, many people are all too prone to letting imagination fill in the uncertain details lacking in hasty observation so that the bird comes to resemble the illustration in the book. Wishful thinking can sometimes be highly misleading in this way. But it is possible to train oneself to identify wild birds so as to reduce this danger and make sure that the identification fits the illustrations and descriptions in the books. Somebody who has not trained himself to identify birds in the field will make mistakes when he suddenly wants to know about a bird he has just seen, just like a child who is learning to read guesses at letters, syllables and whole words and so misses a complete understanding of what is being read. In identifying birds in the field, the observer must train his hearing no less than his sight. If an identification is to be made accurately, observations should be recorded in writing, possibly accompanied by a sketch. Even the most inexperienced observer will soon recognize the Snow Bunting (1), the Redwing (2), the Golden Plover (3), the Whimbrel (4), the Mallard (5), the Raven (6) and the Great Black-backed Gull (7).

The body shape of different species varies greatly, as do the various features of their bodies. Some are stoutly-built, such as the Golden Plover (3); others, like the White Wagtail (8) are more slender. The head may be small or large compared

1

2

3

4

5

6

7

with the body (9 and 10). Wings may be sharply pointed, like those of the Arctic Tern (11) or ragged like those of the Eagle (12). Tail shape is a good distinguishing feature. The main tail types are (see the illustrations of tail types): wedge-shaped, like the Raven's; curved, like the Golden Plover's; straight-ended, like the Great Black-backed Gull's; lightly forked, like the Snow Bunting's or deeply forked like the Arctic Tern's. Certain of the tail-feathers may also be distinctive in length, e.g. the Arctic Tern's tail has long edge feathers (11) while that of the Arctic Skua has long central feathers (13). The tail may also be extremely short, like that of the Slavonian Grebe (14).

The beaks or bills of all bird species have developed in accordance with their methods of feeding. In addition to serving as knife, fork and spoon, the beak is used as a comb, weapon, sieve, fishing net and grip. Just as feeding habits differ between species, so does the form of the beak. The White Wagtail (15), which lives on insects, has a narrow beak. The Snow Bunting (16) has a broad short beak for eating seeds. For life on moors and grassland, the Golden Plover (17) is served well by a short, shallow beak, while the Snipe (18), living in marshland, has a long, slender beak. The Arctic Tern (19) has a sharply-pointed dagger-like beak; the Great Black-backed Gull's beak (20) is hooked at the end; the Merlin and Falcon have hooked beaks (21); ducks (22) geese and swans (23) have broad, flat bills with their edges adapted according to whether they sieve their food from mud and water, tear up grass or catch fish (24). The colour of the beak is also a useful feature for identifying birds.

Like beaks, birds' feet and legs have also become adapted to their methods of feeding and other aspects of their lifestyles. Those which feed in marshes and mudflats have long legs (25), and their feet project behind their tails in flight, slightly in the case of the Oystercatcher (26), a long way in the case of the Redshank, and even more on the Whimbrel (27) and the Black-tailed Godwit. The Snow Bunting is short-legged, as this species crouches close to the ground and feeds on seeds. Seabirds have short legs (28). Thus, the length and colour of feet and legs are useful identification features.

In field identification, the observer should pay

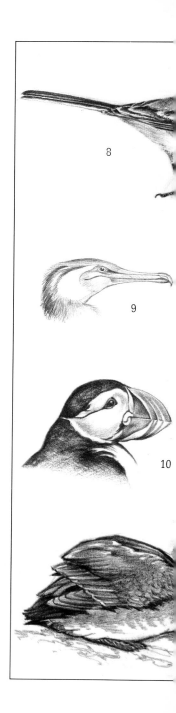

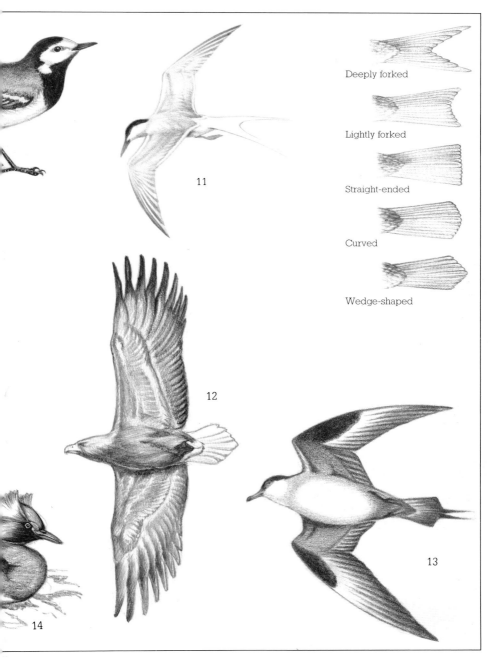

Deeply forked

Lightly forked

Straight-ended

Curved

Wedge-shaped

11

12

13

14

attention to the bird's general behaviour as well as its appearance. Each species has its distinguishing behaviour patterns and movements. The Wren and the Blackbird hold their tails erect (29), as does the Razorbill when swimming. The Wheatear and the Redshank move with jerky bowing movements. Eiders and other ducks rear their heads back. The Red-necked Phalarope turns round continually when swimming.

A bird observed swimming may lie well down in the water like the Cormorant (30), low at the front like ducks and geese (31), have a swimming style resembling that of the Mallard or float lazily along like the Kittiwake (32).

Birds vary in the way they land on water. Some make vertical landings like a helicopter (e.g. the Gulls). Others, such as the ducks, land with their feet extended in front of them (33) or on their bellies with a great deal of splashing, like the Great Northern Diver.

Birds take off from water in one of two ways: suddenly and vertically like a helicopter (34) or with a run and a lot of splashing like a heavy water-plane (35).

Some birds which feed while swimming find their food floating on the surface, and turn circles or dart from side to side as if they were writing on the surface, like the Red-necked Phalarope. Others, like the Mallard (36) up-end themselves. Then there are species which dive by kicking so that they rise above the surface in order to put their bodies under (37). Some flap their wings as they dive, such as the Auks, while others submerge themselves like submarines (the Great Northern Diver and Red-throated Diver).

Some birds gather their food from the surface of the sea in flight (38), hovering, like the Arctic Tern (39) above the water, while the Gannet (40) falls vertically, from heights of up to 30 metres, to catch its prey. Other species gather food from the surface of the water without either hovering or diving.

Various idiosyncrasies in behaviour may be useful in identification. The Redshank struts and bobs up and down, the Wren (29) jerks its tail up and Cormorants stand in a very dignified pose on skerries or shore rocks, gently waving their half-extended wings (41). The Harlequin Duck jerks its head continually while swimming, and raises its tail.

Birds have a great variety of flight styles, so that

15

16

17

18

19

20

21

22

24

23

25

26

27

with practice, the observer can learn to tell them apart with confidence. Does it fly straight like the Redwing? Or in dips like the White Wagtail? Does it flutter like the Snow Bunting (42)? Or fly darting from side to side like the Snipe? Does it flap its wings deeply and with relaxed movements like the Arctic Tern (43)? Or in rapid, shallow flaps like the Golden Plover (44)?

The constant rhythmic wing-beats of the Whimbrel (45) are completely different from the young Fulmar's and the Gannet's (46) alternating bursts of quick flapping and gliding or the flight of the White Wagtail, which often alternates gliding with closed wings with intermittent bursts of flapping in order to increase speed.

Many species can be identified immediately by their colouring alone. Thus the Raven can be recognized by its black colour, both sexes being alike in colour. It would be convenient if the same method could be used with all 70 Icelandic breeding species. In the case of 57 species the sexes are alike, while in the case of the remaining species the sexes have different plumage.

Thirty-six species change the colouring of their plumage to some extent at least twice each year, and the Ptarmigan does so three times a year. In addition to this, the young of all species have plumage which is different from that of the adult bird, and in some cases it takes from three to five years for the young to acquire the adult plumage. Consequently, the bird-watcher who is not closely familiar with the Icelandic breeding species may think that there are more of them than in fact there are. The variety of colours and patterns adds to the richness of the natural environment in Iceland and leads to a greater appreciation of Nature's methods, but it also makes the challenge greater for the bird-watcher. In order to gain a clear knowledge of the colour patterns of birds, it is necessary to know the various parts of birds' bodies so as to be sure of where the colour features are found. A bird may have spots or speckles on its breast, like the Redwing, or on its flanks, like the Common Redpoll. It may be black on its back and upper wings, like the Lesser and Greater Black-backed Gull. The tail may have a special colouring, or the rump may be conspicuously of a single colour; the bird may carry one or more bands or patches on the top or underneath of its wings.

28

Feet adapted for swimming
(Auk family)

Ptarmigan's foot

Webbing between all toes
(Paddlefeet)

Perching foot
(Passerines)

Talons
(Bird of prey)

29

30

31

32

33

35

34

37

36

Colour patterns on the wings are important when it comes to identifying ducks and waders. Stripes above, through or underneath the eye are also key features. The patterns, let alone the colours, in birds' plumage are almost inexhaustible. Why should Nature have developed all these colours, hues and patterns? For communication. Man's aircraft, ships and other vehicles send signals to each other with lights and colours, and we can even communicate by means of flags of different colours and patterns. Birds use essentially the same techniques to establish their identity. There are also parallels between the courtship procedures of birds and Man's hair-styles, manicure, make-up and colours and fashions of dress for the purpose of attracting the opposite sex. All of this adds to the variety and attraction of the natural world for the observer.

Birds in flight make noises which are also useful in identification. Even birds which fly too high to be distinguished easily may sometimes be identified by the sounds they make, as most species have distinct calls. In addition to calls produced in the birds' respiratory systems, some species also produce noises by the interaction of air-currents and certain feathers (e.g. the Snipe and some duck species) and wing-beats can also produce sharp noises (Doves and Pigeons). It is extremely difficult to describe the repertoire of bird calls in the various circumstances of their use, but attempts are made in this book to give as accurate an account as possible of various sounds and calls: sounds of alarm and warning, courting and mating songs and the cries of chicks. The observer is best advised to learn these sounds in the field, though recordings can often be of help too.

The challenge of mastering all this knowledge may seem deterring for the beginning bird-watcher, but anyone who tries to tackle it will be intrigued by the variety of colours, shapes, movements and calls. And those who persevere soon find that they can most often give the answer to the question: "What sort of bird is that?"

38

44

39

40

41

42

43

45

46

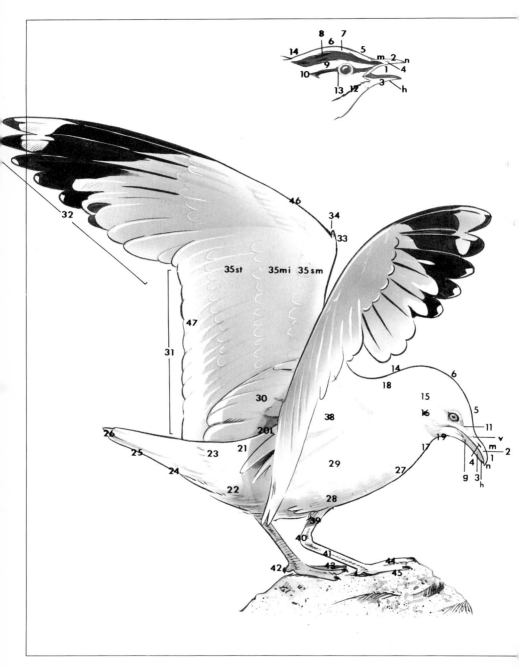

Parts of a Bird

1	Bill	30	Scapulars
m	Culmen	31	Secondaries
n	Nail	32	Primaries
v	Cere	33	Carpal joint
h	Gonys	34	Alula
2	Upper mandible		
3	Lower mandible		
4	Nostril	**Upperwing**	
5	Forehead		
6	Crown	35	Upperwing coverts
8	Lateral crown-stripe	sm	Lesser coverts
9	Supercilium	mi	Median coverts
10	Eye-stripe	st	Greater coverts
11	Lore	36	Speculum
12	Moustachial stripe		
13	Eye-ring		
14	Nape	**Underwing**	
15	Ear-converts (cheek)		
16	Cheek	37	Underwing coverts
17	Foreneck	sm	Median coverts
18	Hindneck	st	Greater coverts
19	Chin, throat	38	Axillaries
20-H	Mantle	39	Tibia (thigh)
20-L	Back		
21	Rump	40	Knee
22	Vent	41	Tarsus
23	Uppertail coverts	42	Hind toe
24	Undertail coverts	43	Inner toe
25	Outer tail feathers	44	Middle toe
26	Central tail feathers	45	Outer toe
27	Breast	46	Front margin of wing
28	Belly	47	Hind margin of wing
29	Flank		

Photographs Preceding Each Section

The photographs preceding the main sections of this guide have been chosen to illustrate the typical habitats of the birds described in each section.

P. 29: Sea birds nest in their thousands in sheer cliffs like these, in the Westman Islands off the south coast. Photo: Sigurgeir Jónasson.

P. 53: Waders on the mudflats near Hjörsey, Mýrasýsla. Mudflats are among the most important staging areas for waders on their migratory journeys in the spring and autumn. Photo: Kristinn Haukur Skarphéðinsson.

P. 87: The view from Ámýrarklettar, Bjarnarhafnarfjall, on the Snæfellsnes Peninsula. This is a large breeding ground for the Glaucous Gull. Gulls, skuas and terns nest in dense colonies near the sea or lakes, their main sources of food. Photo: Kristinn Haukur Skarphéðinsson.

P. 113: Feral Pigeons in flight over central Reykjavík. In urban areas, this species nests on buildings, whereas the other dove and pigeon species found in Iceland favour trees and bushes. Photo: Jóhann Óli Hilmarsson.

P. 121: A Tufted Duck, with ducklings, and a female Wigeon on Lake Mývatn. Ducks and other waterfowl nest in dense vegetation near rivers, lakes and the sea, and soon after hatching the young follow their mothers out onto the water. Photo: Rafn Hafnfjörð.

P. 171: Hrísey, in the north of Iceland, has one of the highest densities of breeding Ptarmigan. The birds are unafraid and come close to houses. Ptarmigan nest in heather and scrub. Photo: Dr Finnur Guðmundsson.

P. 175: An eagle in flight, one of the rarer but most rewarding sights which can greet the bird-watcher. Birds of prey and owls nest in mountain crags, rough lava, woodland and on small islands. Photo: Magnús Magnússon.

P. 185: Starlings converge on towns to nest in roofs and housetops, feeding and spending the night in trees and gardens. Many passerines nest in trees, which also provide them with food, berries being an important part of their diet in late summer and autumn. Photo: Jóhann Óli Hilmarsson.

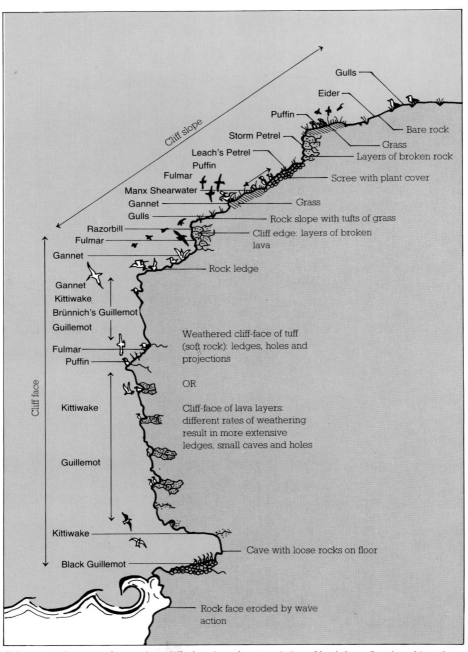

Schematic diagram of a nesting cliff, showing characteristics of both lava (hard rock) and palagonite (soft rock) cliffs and typical nest sites of various species.

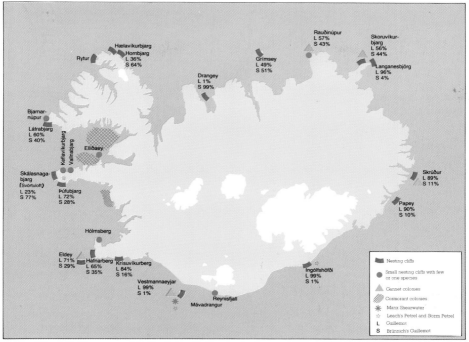

Ratio (%) of Guillemot and Brünnich's Guillemot in the numbers of these species in various nesting cliffs 1939–1979 (Þorsteinn Einarsson 1979).

Typical island nesting site in Breiðafjörður.

Seabirds

Fourteen species of seabirds are listed below. Various other species are also closely connected with the sea, but they do not fulfil the following criteria which characterize seabirds:

1. They derive all their food from the sea.
2. Their nesting grounds are by the sea.
3. They live all their lives on the sea except for the time spent on their nesting grounds.

Other features which seabirds have in common include:

— they are relatively long-lived,
— they mate for life,
— they keep to the same nesting grounds,
— they generally lay a single egg, except for the Black Guillemot, the Shag and the Cormorant, and
— they mostly lay eggs in colonies.

However, seabirds differ in physical structure, e.g. in the shape of their legs and beaks. Those differences reflect different feeding adaptions; some species catch their food on the surface of the sea while swimming or in flight while others dive or swim under water to catch fish or other creatures on the sea-bed. The 14 species fall into the following groups:

1. **Procellariidae** (Tubenoses — the nostrils form a tube or pipe on the top of the beak): the Manx Shearwater and the Fulmar (double tube), Leach's Petrel and the Storm Petrel (single tube).
2. **Sulidae and Phalacrocoracidae** (Paddlefeet — with webbing between all the toes): the Gannet, Cormorant and Shag.
3. **Alcidae** (Auks and the Puffin — with black and white feathers): the Razorbill, Guillemot, Brünnich's Guillemot, the Little Auk, the Black Guillemot and the Puffin.

The nesting cliffs marked on the map on page 26 are those where eggs have traditionally been gathered or birds caught for food. It is thought that of the North Atlantic stocks of auks and puffins, which are estimated as numbering about 90 million birds, some 20 million come each year to the coasts of Iceland and its outlying islands. The largest and most densely populated nesting cliffs are those of the Vestfirðir. Iceland's first settlers turned to the nesting cliffs for meat when there was little to be had from their flocks and herds of domestic animals, and ever since, they have been a source of fresh meat and eggs in early spring, the feathers of the butchered birds were collected and their innards dried and used as fuel.

Manx Shearwater

Puffinus puffinus   1

30–38 cm — Breeder — Sexes identical — 4

Long-winged and short-tailed medium-sized seabird with black upperparts and white underparts. Mottled-brown on dark parts and grey on light parts. Dark wing and tail-borders below, broadest on primaries. Dark and slender, hook-tipped bill with tubular nostrils. Flesh-coloured legs with grey-blue margins. Brownish-black eyes. *Juv* and *ad* are indistinguishable. — Usually gregarious. Alternates in flight between periods of wing flapping and banking and gliding on long, narrow, stiff wings low over water, often in flocks, alternately showing black upperparts and white underparts. Takes food while swimming, also by hovering with paddling feet or by plunging and diving. Does not follow ships. **Vo:** Silent at sea, but utters various weird caws, crows and screams in colonies. **Hab:** Oceanic and only seen on land when breeding. Breeds locally in dense colonies on turf-topped islands, often with Puffins and petrels. Nocturnal in colonies; seen in huge flocks nearby in the evening. Often seen offshore. Winter in S-Atlantic, west to S-America. **Bre:** Nests in burrows or (rarely) rock crevices. Burrows can be up to 2 m long with a chamber, lined with dry grass and other vegetative matter at the end. Lays one egg, usually in May; incubation and fledging periods are long. **Dist:** Common in Vestmannaeyjar, the only known breeding area in Iceland. **I:** Skrofa.

1. White below, except for dark wing and tail-borders.
2. Sooty-black above.
3. Dark bill and crown.

Sooty Shearwater

Puffinus griseus   2

40–51 cm — Summer visitor — Sexes identical — 5

Sooty-brown seabird, except for whitish linings on underwings. — Heavy-bodied and narrow-winged with small head and long slender bill. Glides close to waves like other shearwaters. Occasionally follows ships. **Vo:** Silent at sea. **Hab:** Oceanic, sometimes seen inshore. **Dist:** Breeds in the Southern Hemisphere, visitor to the N-Atlantic during the austral winter. Occurs in Icelandic waters May to November, most common in August - September, particularly off the south coast. **I:** Gráskrofa.

1. Sooty-brown above and below.
2. Pale centre of underwings.
3. Dark and slender bill.

Manx Shearwater.

Sooty Shearwater.

Leach's Petrel

Oceanodroma leucorhoa 3

19–22 cm — Breeder — Sexes identical — 2

Small, dark-brown seabird. Pale-grey diagonal bar on upperwing, no underwing marks. Rump white, divided in middle by (sometimes indistinct) grey stripe. Forked tail. *Ad* and *juv* alike. Black bill, eyes and feet. — Flight is buoyant, with constant changes in speed and direction. Legs drooping in flight. Compared with smaller Storm Petrel has longer and more pointed wings, also different flight pattern. Does not follow ships. **Vo:** Usually silent at sea. Heard nocturnally at breeding grounds. Flight call is chattering, staccato notes. Burrow call is churring with wheezing notes and interrupted by flight call. **Hab:** Strictly pelagic, except in breeding season. Breeds in dense colonies on islands and headlands. Nocturnal in colonies, only seen by day when feeding at sea or driven ashore by autumn storms. **Bre:** Mostly in burrows dug in soft soil, often with Puffins, Manx Shearwaters and Storm Petrels. The tunnel, up to 2 m long, has an enlarged nest chamber at end, little nesting material. Lays one egg in May-July, mainly June. **Dist:** The known colonies are in Vestmannaeyjar and Ingólfshöfði. Population estimate is 50,000-100,000 pairs. Winters in southern seas. **I:** Sjósvala.

1. *White rump with grey centre stripe. Forked tail.*
2. *Grey bars on upperwings.*
3. *Black legs, drooping in flight.*

Storm Petrel

Hydrobates pelagicus 4

14–18 cm — Breeder — Sexes identical — 1

The smallest Icelandic seabird. Similar to Leach's Petrel in apperance and behaviour. Sooty-brown plumage, darker above. White band on underwing variable in size. White rump curves down to vent. Slightly rounded or square tail. Black bill and legs. Dark-brown eyes. *Ad* and *juv* alike. — Fluttering and weak flight with short glides; patters with feet on surface with raised wings. Sometimes follows ships. Told from Leach's Petrel by smaller size, different tail-shape, no marks on rump or upperwings, shorter wings and different flight pattern. **Vo:** Silent at sea but heard nocturnally in colonies. Voice distinctive from Leach's. So called "flight" call is a low 'terr-chick'. In burrows utters a purring, harsh 'arrr-r-r' with equally spaced 'hiccoughing' breath-notes. **Hab:** Pelagic, breeds in colonies on islands and headlands. Nocturnal at breeding grounds but seen during the day feeding over the ocean surface. **Bre:** Nests mainly in narrow crevices in lava and cliffs or under boulders on scree slopes. Little nesting material. One egg, laid June to August, mainly mid-June to mid-July. **Dist:** Same as Leach's Petrel. Winter S-Atlantic. **I:** Stormsvala.

1. *Pale underwing-band.*
2. *Square tail. Clear white rump.*
3. *Black legs, drooping in flight.*

Leach's Petrel.

Storm Petrel.

Fulmar
Fulmarus glacialis **5**

1. *Rounded head, short and stout neck.*
2. *Yellowish bill, tubular nostrils.*
3. *Bluish-grey wings, white patches on primaries.*

45–50 cm — Breeder — Sexes identical — 5

A large, stocky petrel resembling a gull. Head, neck and underparts white or tinged with yellow, contrasting with grey back and upperwings. Dark-brown primaries with light patch on inner primaries. Greyish flanks, tail and rump. Grey underwing with darker edges. Rounded head and short neck. Northern dark phase, 'Blue Fulmars' have uniformly smoky or dark-grey plumage. Bill is short and thick with a hooked tip and tubed nostrils. *Ad* and *juv* alike. Dark-brown eyes. Bluish or greenish legs. — Easily distinguished from gulls by flight pattern: beats narrow wings fast several times, then glides on stiff wings. Floats high on water when swimming. Takes off with difficulty, leaping on water. Habitually follows ships. **Vo:** Rather silent at sea; chuckling and grunting notes when feeding. At nest various guttural cackling or grunting calls 'ag-ag-ag-arrr'. **Hab:** Pelagic. Breeds in colonies on cliffs on islands, coasts and inland. Also on top of steep, rocky islands and stacks. Travels widely in North Atlantic during non-breeding season, visiting colonies when weather is mild. **Bre:** The nest, usually a shallow hollow, often lined with pebbles or dead vegetation, is placed on a ledge or in a cave or a crevice. One egg laid, mainly in May. **Dist:** Now very common in coastal regions in all parts of Iceland, also widely distributed in inland localities, up to 50 km from the coast. **Rem:** In the 17th century the only known Fulmar colonies in Iceland were on Grímsey and Eldey islands. Since then the population has increased and spread tremendously; this is still continuing. Eggs, adults and young were harvested for food (still in some regions) and fat for salve and fuel in earlier times. Fulmars have always been unpopular with fowlers because of the stomach-oil they regurgitate when disturbed. Dark-phase-birds are frequently seen in Fulmar flocks offshore, up to 10% on the fishing banks off the North coast. The scientific name of the species, *Fulmarus*, stems from the old Icelandic name *fúlmár*, meaning foul gull. **I:** Fýll.

Fulmar.

Fulmars in colony.

Gannet

Sula bassana 6

87–100 cm — Breeder — Sexes identical — 7

Large, white seabird. *Ad* white with yellow-tinged head and neck, and black wing tips (primaries and primary coverts) on long, pointed wings. Black base of bill and gular stripe unfeathered. Long, wedge-shaped tail. Long, pointed grey bill with dark lines. Blue-grey eye-ring and pale-yellow eyes. Grey-black legs with greenish linings. *Imm* variable, ranging from blackish (*juv*) to pied; acquires *ad* plumage in 4th year, easily identified by distinctive "cigar-shape" and characteristic actions. — Powerful flight with deep wing-beats, mixed with glides on angled wings. Dives vertically after fish, plunging headlong from up to 40 m height with wings folded back. Air sacs under skin on the breast protect Gannets when they strike the water. Floats rather high on water when swimming. **Vo:** Noisy in colonies, uttering guttural croaks or grunts and a barking 'arrah'. **Hab:** Oceanic. Breeds in dense colonies on rocky stacks, islands and coastal cliffs (fig. p. 25). Few seen inshore during non-breeding season, mainly *ads;* younger birds disperse. **Bre:** Makes a large nest of seaweed and other available material, cemented together with mud and excrements on broad ledges or on top of islands or stacks. One egg, laid March to May, usually April. **Dist:** At present, 5 colonies (colonies on 4 of the Vestmannaeyjar are counted as 1) are occupied in Iceland and 5 historic colonies have been deserted. Icelandic Gannets winter in N-Atlantic, recoveries of ringed birds come from Greenland and Norway south to NW-Africa. **Rem:** A recent count (1983–84) gave a world population of 213,000 pairs of which 23,000 pairs (10.8%) belonged to the Icelandic population. The largest colony is on Eldey (fig. p. 25) off the SW coast, with 14,500 pairs counted in 1985. Gannets, mainly nestlings, were formerly harvested in large numbers. **I:** Súla.

1. Long, pointed, blue-grey bill.
2. Long, pointed wings with black ends.
3. Yellow tinge on head and upper-neck.

Second summer.

36

Gannets, adults with young.

Gannet plunging.

Cormorant

Phalacrocorax carbo 7

80–100 cm — Breeder — Sexes identical — 7

Large, dark seabird with long neck. *Ad* in breeding plumage has white cheeks and chin, also white patch on thighs. Rest of body is glossy bluish-black, duller in winter. *Imm* brownish above and lighter below. Mostly dark bill with hooked tip, unfeathered yellow skin at base. Bluish-green eyes. Black legs. — Flies with extended neck and slightly raised head. Often perches with wings hanging open. Easily confused with Shag and divers, but distinguished from Shag by larger size, heavier bill, and larger head with flat, not rounded, crown which is angled at nape. **Vo:** In breeding grounds variable, deep, guttural notes 'rr-rah', otherwise silent. **Hab:** Marine; breeds on islands, skerries and rocks. Winters in coastal waters. Sometimes seen inland. **Bre:** Colonial; nests made of seaweed and lined with grass and feathers, placed on top of sparsely vegetated islands and skerries. Clutch, 3–5 eggs, laid in April and May. **Dist:** Nearly all colonies are in Breiðafjörður and Faxaflói, decreasing or disappearing elsewhere. In winter found all along the coast. **I:** Dílaskarfur.

1. Heavy, hook-tipped and mostly dark bill.
2. Pale cheeks and chin, naked yellow gape-patch.
3. Immatures pale below.

Immature.

Shag

Phalacrocorax aristotelis 8

65–80 cm — Breeder — Sexes identical — 7

Large, dark seabird. *Ad* is green-glossed black during breeding season, duller and browner in winter. Upcurved crest on forecrown from January to spring. Scaly above due to purpled feather edges. Black legs. *Imm* dark-brown with white throat, paler on belly. Black bill, browner in *imm,* yellow gape-patch. Green (*ad*) or yellow (*imm*) eyes. Black legs. — Behaviour and appearance similar to Cormorant but not as shy; build smaller and slender, with thinner bill, more rounded head, steeper forehead and slender neck, flies with faster wing-beats, neck more straight and keeps lower over water. Perched keeps wings at smaller angle from body than Cormorant. Dives with a forward spring. **Vo:** Vocal mainly in colonies, utters grunting and hissing notes and loud throat-clicking. **Hab:** Marine, breeds in colonies on low islands, skerries and coastal cliffs. Coastal in winter, never seen inland. **Bre:** Nest structure similar to Cormorant. Clutch of 1–6 eggs, but usually three, laid late April through May. **Dist:** Main colonies are in Breiðafjörður, but found elsewhere on the west coast. Winters mostly in same general area. **I:** Toppskarfur.

1. Dark-grey bill, yellow gape-patch.
2. Upcurved crest on breeding ads.
3. Imm darker below than Cormorant.

Cormorant in breeding plumage.

Shags in breeding plumage.

Razorbill

Alca torda

37–39 cm — Breeder — Sexes identical — 4

Large alcid, in *summer* with black head, neck and back, white
breast and belly. Upperwing black, underwing coverts white,
primaries dark, also secondaries, but with white tips showing as
white line on folded wing. Black bill, flattened laterally, white
line across near tip and narrow white line extending from base
of bill to eye. In *winter* plumage with white throat, chin and
ear-coverts, brown around eyes and duller bill-marks. *Juv*
browner and with smaller all-dark bill. Black eyes and legs. —
Bill and long pointed tail often held raised when swimming.
Small narrow wings. Flight fast and straight, low over water.
Brakes with feet outstretched on land or water. Swims buoyantly.
Uses legs and wings when diving. Sits on tarsi and balances with
tail. Size and pattern resembles Guillemot and Brünnich's
Guillemot but thicker with shorter neck. **Vo:** At breeding
grounds a deep or shrill grunt 'urrr' or a weak whistle. **Hab:**
Marine, both inshore and offshore. Breeds in colonies on coastal
cliffs or on scree slopes. **Bre:** One egg laid in May or June,
mainly in crevices or under boulders, also on bare rock on
ledges. **Dist:** On bird-cliffs around Iceland. Wintering areas are
little known, some stay in Icelandic waters but it is assumed that
most migrate. Only recoveries are from the Faroes. **I:** Álka.

Summer:
1. *Deep, black bill, flattened laterally.*
   White vertical and horizontal lines on
   bill and forehead.
2. *White line on folded wing.*

Winter:
White on belly and breast
extends to eyes.

Razorbills, summer.

Razorbills (in front) and Guillemots (behind). The Guillemot in the middle is the bridled form.

Little Auk
Alle alle

10

17–19 cm — Winter visitor/Rare breeder — Sexes identical — 2

The smallest and least common auk. In *summer* black above down to breast with dark underwings. Other parts white. White streaks on scapulars. White-tipped secondaries form a thin wing-bar. White spot above eyes. In *winter* white breast, throat and cheeks, tinged dark and dark smudge on sides of neck. Stubby, conical black bill. Dark-brown eyes. Dark-grey legs, black webs. — Found single or in small parties. Chubby build, tiny bill and small size (as Starling) distinctive. Looks almost neckless in flight or on water. More agile than other auks. Usually swims low in water with tail slightly upcurved, but when resting floats high. **Vo:** Silent except on breeding grounds. High and shrill chattering notes heard in colonies. **Hab:** Oceanic; breeds among boulders on scree slopes beneath cliffs. Seen in coastal waters in winter, often accompanying drift ice. **Bre:** One egg, laid in May- June in crevices on cliffs or among boulders on screes. **Dist/Rem:** The Little Auk is almost extinct as a breeder in Iceland. Few pairs still linger on in Grímsey and are strictly protected. Formerly more common on the north coast, but milder climate during this century presumably caused its decline. Little Auks from Greenland and other Arctic countries observed in varying numbers every winter, especially in northern and eastern parts of the country. Sometimes found driven ashore in large numbers on coasts and inland after northern winter gales. **I:** Haftyrðill.

Summer:
1. *Short, conical, black bill.*
2. *Black head, throat, neck and upper breast.*
3. *White lines on black scapulars.*

Winter:
White on belly and lower breast extends up to cheeks, black smudge on neck sides.

Little Auks, summer.

Little Auks, summer.

Guillemot

Uria aalge 11

38–41 cm — Breeder — Sexes identical — 4

Summer:
1. White below.
2. Blackish-brown above.
3. Dark streaks on flanks.

One of the most common cliff-breeding auks. In *summer* blackish-brown above and white below. Dark streaks and smudges on upper flanks distinctive. White tips of dark secondaries form white line on folded wing. 'Bridled' form has white ring around eye and white line extending back from ring (see photo p. 41). In *winter* white of breast extends to chin, neck-sides and cheeks, divided by black downcurved stripe behind eyes. Narrow, sharp-pointed, black bill. Black eyes. Black base colour of legs. — Acts and habits similar to Razorbill and Brünnich's Guillemot. Highly gregarious. Flies with retracted neck. Best distinguished from Brünnich's at good range by streaked sides, all dark bill, slightly browner upperparts and less white on sides of rump. **Vo:** A long harsh growl 'arra' and trumpeting moans when calling young from ledges. **Hab:** Oceanic, seen both inshore and offshore. Breeds in colonies on coastal cliffs and on top of stacks and islands. **Bre:** No nest, lays one egg on bare ledges, May – June. **Dist:** Bird cliffs around the coast. Winter areas not well known, some stay in coastal waters but most migrate. **Rem:** The 'bridled' form is relatively most common in the Vestmannaeyjar, slightly more than 50% of the population. Compared with Brünnich's, the Guillemot is more common on bird cliffs in the south than on the north coast (fig. p. 27). For centuries Guillemot, Brünnich's Guillemot, Razorbill and Puffin have been harvested for food (adults and eggs), feathers and fat for fuel. The chicks, accompained by their parents, leave the colonies when they are still unable to fly. A recent population estimate is 1,600,000 pairs. **I:** Langvía.

Winter:
White throat, neck and ear-coverts.
Black line behind eyes.

Guillemot, adult, summer.

Colony of Guillemots.

Brünnich's Guillemot

Uria lomvia   12

39–43 cm — Breeder — Sexes identical — 4

Large black and white alcid, dark above and white below. In *summer* plumage differs from Guillemot by black, rather than brownish-black upperparts and white flanks (no streaks), also white of breast usually rises to a sharper point on foreneck, whiter sides of rump (seen in flight), shorter and thicker bill with white streak on base of upper bill. In *winter* white on chin and throat, but black on head extends well below eyes onto cheeks. White line at base of bill still visible. Other parts as Guillemot. — Habits like Guillemot and Razorbill. **Vo:** Purring and murmuring, similar to Guillemot. **Hab:** Similar to Guillemot, though more oceanic in winter. Nests in colonies on coastal cliffs. **Bre:** Arrives later at colonies than Guillemot, and therefore often settles on narrower ledges and outcrops (fig. p. 26). Lays one egg on bare ledge in May-June. **Dist:** Breeds on all major bird-cliffs, though mainly on the north coast. Winter grounds not well known, probably mainly in N-Atlantic. Birds from High Arctic colonies winter in Icelandic waters. Less common inshore in winter than Guillemot. **Rem:** The population size has been estimated 2 million pairs. **I:** Stuttnefja.

Summer:
1. *Narrow white streak on base of upper mandible.*
2. *White flanks.*
3. *Black above, white line on folded wing.*

Winter:
White throat and chin, black crown stretching well below eyes.

46

Brünnich's Guillemots, summer.

Black Guillemot
Cepphus grylle

Adult, summer:
1. *Black bill. Red gape and tongue.*
2. *Black body, except for large white patch on wing-coverts and white underwing with black borders.*
3. *Red legs.*

30–32 cm — Breeder — Sexes identical — 4

The only alcid with black underparts. All black in *summer* plumage, except for large, oval, white patch on wing-coverts and white underwing with black borders. Short, pointed, black bill, vermilion red gape and tongue. Dark-brown eyes. Red legs. In *winter* paler than other auks, barred black or dark-grey above, mottled white below. Black tail. White patch on dark wings less obvious. Yellowish legs. *Juv* more grey-brown mottled above, with scattering of grey in wing patches and dark crown. *First summer* has dark lines on wing panels and dark legs. — Action similar to Guillemot, but more agile on land. Found single or in small groups. Flies with rapid, whirring wing-beats low over water, wing patterns obvious. **Vo:** A metallic peep or shrill whistling 'speee...'. **Hab:** Marine; breeds colonially or single on headlands, islands and coastal cliffs. Coastal in winter. **Bre:** Two eggs are laid in May-June in rock holes, in screes, under boulders and on ledges in caves. **Dist:** Breeds all around the country. About 1/3 of the population, mainly *imm,* winters in Greenland, rest of the birds are residents. Some Black Guillemots from High Arctic colonies winter in Icelandic waters. **Rem:** Like other alcids, the Black Guillemot was formerly harvested for meat and eggs. **I:** Teista.

Juvenile, winter:
Barred black or dark-grey above, mottled white below. Wing patches less obvious than in summer.

Adult, winter.

Black Guillemot, adult, summer.

Black Guillemot, juvenile, winter.

Puffin

Fratercula arctica   **14**

29–31 cm — Breeder — Sexes identical — 3

The most common Icelandic seabird. *Ad* in *summer* plumage
black above and white below, black crown and black collar on
foreneck. Black underwing. Grey cheeks. Colourful large
triangular bill with horny plates. Blue-grey, red and yellow
lateral stripes, and grooves on bill get deeper and more
colourful with age. Yellow, bare skin at corner of mouth. Horn
plates around yellow eye and dark line behind it. Red legs. In
winter cheeks darker, without dark line and plates around eye,
and horn plates on bill are moulted, so bill becomes smaller and
duller; orange to yellow legs. *Juv* similar to *ad* in winter but
cheek and lore darker. Much smaller, all-dark bill. Pinkish legs.
— Highly gregarious. Smaller and more compact compared with
Razorbill and the guillemots, also different head shape and no
wing bars. Stands upright and walks without difficulty. **Vo:**
Usually silent, but in breeding grounds utters deep growling
notes 'arr-ow-er', both from burrows and when perched in
colonies. **Hab:** Marine; breeds in colonies on islands, headlands
and coastal cliffs. Oceanic in winter. **Bre:** One egg is laid in May
in a burrow dug in turf on slopes, on top of islands and islets, on
grassy ledges but also nests among boulders in screes and in
rock crevices. Little or no nesting material added to scrape.
Dist: Breeds in suitable habitat all around the country. First
winter Puffins winter off Newfoundland but older birds in the
N-Atlantic south and southwest of Iceland south to the Azores.
Puffins seen off the North coast in winter are mainly of
Norwegian origin. **Rem:** The Puffin population in Iceland has a
long history of human exploitation, and the Puffin is currently the
most heavily utilized seabird. In the 19th century the population
declined in many areas and some of the catching methods were
condemned as brutal. In 1875 the Puffin pole-net was first
introduced to Vestmannaeyjar from the Faroes, following a
prohibition of most of the older trapping methods. Pole-netting is
now the main catching method. The netters catch mainly
immatures, as these have a habit of circling the colonies. In
Vestmannaeyjar c. 10% of the catch are adults. The catching is
now considered to be in balance with the Puffin population. The
population size has been estimated at 5–6 million breeding pairs.
I: Lundi.

Adult, summer:
1. *Colourful, triangular, laterally flattened bill.*
2. *Grey cheeks, horn plates around eye.*
3. *Red legs. The only auk not resting on the tarsi.*

Adult, winter and juvenile:
Darker cheeks, duller bill (uniformly dark on juv) and legs; lacks horn plates around eyes and on bill.

Puffin, adult, summer.

Puffin, newly-fledged young.

Waders

Many people find it surprising that ornithologists group the waders or shorebirds together with gulls and auks, but the relationship becomes clear if we compare their anatomical characteristics. Different adaptations have led to such divergence among them that many people are amazed to find that gulls, circling in flight and filling the air with harsh cries, auks, squatting on cliff sills with their low growling noises and the plover in the field with its thin piping call are all close relatives of one another. Under this general heading of waders are treated the 14 species which nest in Iceland as well as the Water Rail, the Coot, five species which are either winter visitors to Iceland or visit the country almost every year as vagrants, and three regular passage visitors, making a total of 24 species.

The common features of waders are long legs and narrow beaks. Their habitat covers coastal regions, marshes, moorland and gravel flats, and areas covered by heather and low bushes. Waders spread northwards in the breeding season and move further south in the winter. The waders are gregarious outside the breeding season and in spring and autumn they can be seen moving in huge flocks whose unanimity and integration of movement is amazing. This is achieved by rhythmic wing-beats which the birds are able to conform to thanks to their ultra-sensitive hearing. Waders build simple nests. Immediately after hatching out, the young leave the nests and fend for themselves, under the supervision of the parent birds. The Oystercatcher and the Snipe are an exception in that they feed their chicks. Feather colouring varies according to the nesting environment. More than other species, waders will feign injury and show alarm in order to distract predators from the vicinity of their nests.

The Phalaropidae, the Red-necked and Grey Phalaropes, form a subfamily of the waders. They are migrants and stay in Iceland for two or three months, after which they fly to the central South Atlantic where uppwelling waters provide them with a plentiful food supply. Both species have lobed toes and particularly dense plumage. The female is more colourful and also more promiscuous, and females compete for the attention of the males, which incubate the eggs and rear the young. The rails and waterhens are included with the waders: the body is flat-sided and there are pads on the long toes, which are adapted for walking on pond and marsh vegetation. The wings are short and the tail short and erect. The Water Rail flies in short bursts, with the feet dangling down conspicuously. Until recently the Water Rail nested in Iceland and was probably a permanent resident, but no nests have been found in recent years. Two related species, the Spotted Crake and Corncrake, which are both smaller, have also been found in Iceland. The Coot is a regular visitor, mostly in the winter. It has been known to nest in Iceland, but never successfully.

Herons resemble the waders in that they are long-necked and long-legged marsh-birds. However, this resemblance reflects adaptations to similar environments but not phylogenic relation. They fly with slow flapping of their broad wings with their necks drawn in and their heads resting on their shoulders. Some heron species occur as vagrants, but only one, the Grey Heron, is sighted regularly. For convenience, it is included here with the true Waders.

53

Golden Plover

Pluvialis apricaria

26–29 cm — Breeder — Sexes similar — 3

The characteristic wader of dry uplands. In *summer* plumage upperparts are speckled golden-yellow and black, underparts blackish: black face, throat, foreneck, breast and belly. White stripe runs from forehead to vent, almost meeting at breast, divides black underparts and white upperparts. White underwings and axillaries, pale wing-bar, yellowish rump. Tail uniform with rest of upperparts. *Winter* and *juv* underparts not black but flecked golden-brown on face and breast, *juv* paler and duller, more distinctly spotted. Black bill, dark grey legs and brown eyes. — Compact build, thick neck, and short, stout bill. Flies rapidly and powerfully, runs and tilts when feeding. Display flight with slow, deep wing-beats distinctive. On breeding territory often stands upright and sings. Gregarious outside breeding season. **Vo:** Display call a melodious whistle 'tloo-ii', alarm call a melancholy 'pluuh'. Flight song a variable trilling and mournful repetition of the phrase 'tirr-pee-oo' followed by 'perpuurlya'. The song has long been regarded as the harbinger of spring in Iceland. **Hab:** Prefers heathland, both

Summer:
1. *Continous black from eyes to belly.*
2. *White stripe divides black lowerparts from yellow upperparts. White axillaries.*
3. *Speckled yellow and black above.*

In winter.

Winter and juvenile plumage: Golden-brown on face and breast, white belly.

at high and low altitudes, also found breeding in other habitats, e.g. on sparsely vegetated gravel flats, in lava fields, peatland, etc. Outside breeding season in flocks in tidal areas and on farmland. **Bre:** Nest an open scrape in low vegetation. Clutch of 4 eggs laid mid-May to July. **Dist:** Common in suitable habitats. Winters in Western Europe (British Isles, France, Spain and Portugal). Some few reach North Africa. **Rem:** Breeding density max. recorded 40 pairs/sq.km but 15–20 pairs/sq.km, seems common in lowland areas. **I:** Heiðlóa.

Golden Plover, summer.

Golden Plover, juvenile.

Grey Plover
Pluvialis squatarola 16

27–30 cm — Vagrant — Sexes similar — 3

Resembles Golden Plover, but can always be identified by grey appearance, white rump and black-barred tail, conspicuous wing-bars and black axillaries. In *summer* with black underparts but unlike Golden Plover with black flanks and white rear belly. In *winter* brown-grey above, *ad* largely white below, *juv* streaked on face, breast and flanks. Blackish-grey bill and legs, dark eyes. **Vo:** Call is a three-noted whistle 'plee-ui-ii'. **Hab:** Usually seen single or occasionally in small flocks on shore, often with Golden Plovers or other waders. **Dist:** Observed in all seasons, but most sightings from Southwest in autumn and winter (September-December). **I:** Grálóa.

Winter (juvenile):
1. *Grey-mottled back.*
2. *White rump. White tail with dark bars.*
3. *Conspicuous pale wing-bars, black axillaries.*

In winter.

Ringed Plover
Charadrius hiaticula 17

18–20 cm — Breeder/Passage migrant — Sexes similar — 2

Small, active wader. Greyish brown above, on crown, back and upperwings; white wing bars. White breast and belly. White-edged dark tail and rump. Distinctive face and breast pattern, *ad* in *summer* with black mask, from bill back to ear coverts, white forehead, white neck-collar and broad black breast band. In *winter* black colour more faded. *Juv* has brown head-marks and breast-band and scaly upperparts. Orange bill with black tip, all black on *juv*. Orange legs. Brown eyes. — Appears long-winged and flies fast and low with regular wing-beats. **Vo:** Call a soft and melodious 'poo-lee' or 'too-eep'. Song starts slowly, then rises and becomes a trilling, repeated note 'too weddee-too weddee'. **Hab:** Breeds on sandy areas and gravel flats on coast and inland. Outside breeding season on coastal mudflats and sandy shores. **Bre:** Nest a shallow open scrape in ground, lined with small stones and pieces of shells. Clutch of 4 eggs laid mid-May to June. Distraction display of breeders towards humans and other potential predators conspicuous. **Dist:** Common breeder in suitable habitats. High Arctic passage migrants stage on Icelandic shores in spring and autumn. Winters probably mainly in W-Africa and SW-Europe. **Rem:** Breeding density can be high, up to 90 pairs/sq.km on coastal gravel flats. **I:** Sandlóa.

Summer:
1. *Black-tipped, orange bill.*
2. *White neck-collar and black breast-band.*
3. *Orange feet.*
4. *Grey-brown above, white below.*

Grey Plover, juvenile.

Ringed Plover in summer.

Oystercatcher

Haematopus ostralegus

40–45 cm — Breeder — Sexes identical — 4

Summer:
1. *Long and stout orange-red bill.*
2. *Black upperparts, except for white wing-bars, rump and base of tail.*
3. *White underparts.*
4. *Pinkish legs.*

Unmistakable large pied black and white wader. Black head and neck down to breast, mantle and upperwings. White underparts, broad white wing-bar, white rump and lower back, white tail with broad, black tail band. *Winter* and *juv* plumage sometimes with white band on throat. Long and stout, orange-red bill. Red eyes and eye-ring. Pink legs. *Juv* browner with shorter and more pointed bill with dark tip, greyish legs. — Noisy and gregarious. Flies low over water. Display flight observed during breeding season, with bird flying in circles with slow wing-beats while singing. **Vo:** Call a shrill, repeated 'ke-beek' or 'pic-pic'. Alarm call a shrill, short 'beek'. Song a long trill with slow beginning. **Hab:** Breeds mainly in coastal areas, also inland near rivers and lakes, even hayfields and sandy meadows. Winters on shores. **Bre:** Nest is an open scrape in ground, lined with small stones and pieces of shells. Lays 2–4 eggs, in May (- June). **Dist:** Found in coastal areas all over the country, most common in S- and W-Iceland where also nests inland. Has spread to north and east coast during this century. A few thousand winter, mainly in Faxaflói and on the SW coast, but majority migrate to the British Isles. **I:** Tjaldur.

Winter/juvenile with white throat.

Oystercatcher, adult, summer.

Oystercatcher.

Whimbrel

Numenius phaeopus   19

40–42 cm — Breeder — Sexes similar — 4

Large wader with long bill, neck and legs. Grey-brown above,
marked with buff. Brown crown with pale central stripe; dark
eye-stripe. Pale throat, belly and underwings. White rump and
lower back distinctive. Barred tail. Dark-brown, long bill, bent
downwards near tip. Brown eyes. Blue-grey legs, projecting
slightly beyond tail in flight. — Noisy and unshy on breeding
grounds. **Vo:** Tittering 7-note whistle 'ti-ti-ti...'; song a repeated
'teeev' followed by fluty bubbling or trill. **Hab:** Breeds chiefly in
bogs and wet moorland, often where wet and dry areas meet,
also dry heathland, vegetated lava-fields and sparsely vegetated
sandy areas. Rarely seen on shores. **Bre:** Nest is a depression in
low vegetation. Lays 4 eggs late May to June. **Dist:** Common in
lowlands, but scattered in highland areas. With Golden Plover
the characteristic upland wader. Strictly migratory, arrives in
May and departs in July-August. Winters in W-Africa south of
Sahara. **Rem:** Breeding density is high, 6–26 pairs/sq.km.
Commonly seen in flocks before departure. **I:** Spói.

1. *Curved, blue-grey bill.*
2. *Pale and dark head-stripes.*
3. *Long, blue-grey legs, projecting
   slightly beyond tail in flight.*

Curlew

Numenius arquata   20

50–60 cm — Winter visitor/Rare breeder — Sexes similar — 5

Similar to Whimbrel but larger, with longer and more evenly
curved bill, and lacks the head-stripes. — Flight rather gull-like.
Shy and wary. **Vo:** Call a melodic, drawn-out whistle 'courr-lee'
or 'croo-ce', alarm call a fast and hoarse 'hwu-kwu-wu-wu'. Song
a loud, variable trill. **Hab/Dist:** Regular winter visitor in
September-April (August-May) from Scandinavia, occurs all over
the country but mainly in small flocks on southwestern shores
and also in Hornafjörður, SE-Iceland. **Bre/Rem:** Has bred on
Melrakkaslétta, NE-Iceland (1987–90). **I:** Fjöruspói.

1. *Long curved bill, much longer than
   Whimbrel's.*
2. *No stripes on head.*

Whimbrel.

Curlew.

Snipe

Gallinago gallinago

21

25–27 cm — Breeder — Sexes similar — 3

Common, medium sized wader. Rufous, speckled black back and upperwings, head, neck, breast and flanks. Buffish-yellow stripes on back and head. Dark crown and eye-stripes, paler moustachial stripe. White belly, pale underwings. Rufous tail, white-edged and rounded. *Juv* similar to *ad.* Straight, long bill, dark but paler at base, pointed downwards in flight. Brown eyes. Yellowish legs. — Between Jack Snipe and Woodcock in size. Seldom seen at close range. When flushed, calls and flies in low zig-zag pattern, then either climbs up and disappears with rapid wing-beats, or drops down suddenly. "Drumming" display flight characteristic. **Vo:** Call a loud repeated note 'tik', 'tika' or 'chick-ka', screeching hoarse 'cheep' when flushed. The "drumming" sound is made by vibration of outer tail-feathers during steep dives in display flight. **Hab:** Breeds in different kinds of wet and dry lowland habitats, e.g. marshes, boggy moors, heathlands, grassland and brushwood. Winters in small numbers near open streamlets, ditches, effluents from hot springs, etc. **Bre:** Nest is a scrape lined with grass, moss etc., hidden in vegetation. Breeds May-July (sometimes later), mainly in later half of May; 4 eggs. **Dist:** In suitable habitats all over the country. Winters in W-Europe (mainly Ireland). **Rem:** Max. recorded breeding density in Iceland 85–90 pairs/sq.km, but 20–35 probably more common in suitable habitats, lower in drier areas. **I:** Hrossagaukur.

1. *Straight, long bill, pointed down in flight.*
2. *Dark and pale stripes on crown and cheeks.*
3. *Four buffish-yellow stripes on back. Rounded and white-edged tail.*

Drumming Snipe.

Snipe.

Snipe.

Jack Snipe

Lymnocryptes minimus

22

17–19 cm — Vagrant — Sexes identical — 2

Smaller than Snipe and with shorter bill. Head and back pattern similar. Broad, dark stripe on crown. Brighter stripes on back. Wedge-shaped tail, no white edges like Snipe's. — Very hard to flush and difficult to observe on ground. When flushed usually silent, with more direct flight (no zig-zag pattern) and slower wing-beats than Snipe and drops down again quickly. **Vo:** Sometimes a low, weak note heard when flushed. **Hab/Dist:** Winter vagrant, seen September to March (mainly November to February). Less common than Woodcock. Most sightings from S- and SW-Iceland. Seen single or in small groups at similar places as wintering Snipe and Woodcock. **I:** Dvergsnípa.

1. *Striped back.*
2. *Smaller than Snipe and with shorter bill.*
3. *Wedge-shaped tail, no white edges.*

Woodcock

Scolopax rusticola

23

33–35 cm — Vagrant — Sexes identical — 4

Larger and heavier than Snipe. Upperparts red-brown. No obvious stripes on back, but transverse barred underparts and black bars on back of head and neck. Broad rounded wings. Rufous tail with black and white tail band. Dark bill, pointed downwards in flight. Large, dark eyes. Pinkish legs. — In flight short neck and tail prominent, flight path is usually straight. Display flight ("roding") at night, performed by ♂♂. Displaying birds fly above treetops with slow wing-beats, uttering grunting and piping sounds. Solitary and shy. Voice: Usually silent except when "roding": deep croaking '...kwarr...', followed by high pitched 'piss-ip' or 'tsiwick'. **Hab/Br/Dis:** Woodcock is an annual vagrant in Iceland, sightings are from September to July (mainly October to January) from E- to SW-Iceland. In winter it is seen in similar places as Snipe and Jack Snipe, especially if trees are found nearby. In recent years ♂♂ have been recorded most summers in birch and conifer woodlands in most parts of the country, but mainly in NE-Iceland. Breeding has not been proved. **I:** Skógarsnípa.

1. *Transverse barred crown and nape.*
2. *No obvious stripes on back. Larger and heavier than Snipe.*
3. *Stubby, rounded wings.*

Jack Snipe.

Woodcock.

Black-tailed Godwit

Limosa limosa **24**

40–44 cm — Breeder — Sexes similar — 4

A large reddish wader of lowland wetlands. In *summer* chestnut-red on head, neck and breast. Back and wing-coverts grey-brown mottled with black. Belly white, flanks and belly with black bars. Long straight bill, broad white wing-bars and white rump and tail-base above black tail characteristic. *Ad* in *winter* uniform grey-brown above and pale below, resembles winter Bar-tailed Godwit except for wing and tail pattern. *Juv* is buff on neck and breast, more like *ad* summer than winter. Long bill with black tip and yellow base. Brown eyes. Blackish, long legs, trailing beyond tail in flight. — Large, erect wader. Flight fast with rapid beats. Nervous and noisy in breeding grounds. **Vo:** Flight-call a loud and clear repeated 'weeta' or 'reeka', alarm call 'quee-yit' or 'quee'. On breeding grounds variable, repeated, nasal notes, some described like 'keh-wee-weeit' and 'wheddy-whit-too'. **Hab:** Breeds in different types of low-lying wetlands and even heathlands and scrublands some distance from water. Seen in wetland areas, hayfields and on tidal mudflats outside breeding season. **Bre:** Nest is a scrape hidden in vegetation. Clutch of 4 eggs laid late May to June. **Dist:** Formerly only in the Southern Lowlands, but since 1920's has been spreading clockwise around the country, arriving Akureyri c. 1950, Mývatn 1963 and Hérað (E-Iceland) 1970. Range extension still taking place. Strictly migratory. Icelandic Godwits winter in W-Europe (mainly Ireland) south to NW-Africa. Breeding density up to 15–20 pairs/sq.km. **I:** Jaðrakan.

Adult, summer:
1. *Long, straight bill.*
2. *Reddish-brown head, neck and breast.*
3. *White rump and tail with broad black band.*
4. *White wing-bars.*

Bar-tailed Godwit

Limosa lapponica **25**

37–39 cm — Vagrant — Sexes dissimilar — 4

Similar to Black-tailed Godwit; best distinguished from it by slightly upcurved bill, lack of white wing-bar, shorter legs just extending beyond barred tail in flight and white rump extending in wedge up to back. ♂ in *summer* is reddish, similar to Black-tailed Godwit, but ♀ is much duller. Whimbrel-like in *winter* and *juv* plumage, *juv* more streaked on breast than *ad*. Long bill, dark with pink base. Dark-brown eyes. Rather short, bluish-grey legs. — Flight and behaviour like Black-tailed. **Vo:** Usually silent, flight call a quick and nasal 'kirrk-kirrk-kirrk'. **Hab/Dist:** In Iceland almost exclusively seen on tidal mudflats and sandy shores. Annual autumn vagrant, winters frequently, usually seen single or in small flocks on southwestern shores and at Hornafjörður, SE-Iceland August-March (mainly September-November). **I:** Lappajaðrakan.

Juvenile (winter):
1. *Slightly upturned bill.*
2. *No wing-bar.*
3. *Barred tail, white rump.*

Black-tailed Godwit in summer plumage.

Juvenile Bar-tailed Godwit.

Redshank

Tringa totanus

26

27–29 cm — Breeder — Sexes identical — 3

Common, noisy wader of farmland and low-lying wetlands. In *summer* grey-brown above with darker streaks and bars. White, streaked and barred dark-brown on throat, breast and belly. White hind-edges of dark grey-brown wings and white rump and lower-back conspicuous in flight. Dark-barred white tail. Long, reddish bill with black tip. Brown eyes, pale-grey eye-ring. Orange-red legs, projecting beyond tail in flight. In *winter* more uniform above, finely streaked below, grey breast, paler legs. *Juv* more buff above, lightly streaked breast, white belly, more yellowish legs. — Noisy behaviour; in breeding grounds flies off with jerky, shallow wing-beats and drooping wings. Perches on stones and poles, often "bobs" and clicks when nervous. Flight fast. Gregarious. **Vo:** Call a musical and melancholic 'tluu' and down slurred 'tleu-heu-heu'. Alarm call an irritating 'kip-kip-kip' or 'tewk-tewk'. Song is variable, loud and musical yodeling notes like 'toolee' or 'taweoo'. **Hab:** Breeds in marshes and grassland in lowland areas. Observed in non-breeding season on coast, e.g. mudflats, estuaries and rocky shores. **Bre:** Nest is scrape, lined with grass, well hidden in vegetation. Four eggs, laid in later half of May to June. **Dist:** Common breeder in suitable habitats all over the country. A few hundred winter on southwest coasts, but majority migrate to W-Europe, mainly British Isles. **Rem:** Max. recorded breeding density 80 pairs/sq.km, but 10-50 pairs is more common. **I:** Stelkur.

Adult, summer:
1. *Reddish, black-tipped bill.*
2. *Dark-barred, white tail. White rump extending in a triangle to back.*
3. *Dark wings with white wing-bars.*
4. *Orange-red legs, either drooping or projecting beyond tail in flight.*

Wood Sandpiper

Tringa glareola

27

19–21 cm — Vagrant/Rare breeder — Sexes identical — 2

Dark-brown above with white spots. Head, neck and breast finely streaked. Clear, white supercilium. In flight, white rump patch and barred tail, no wing-bars, pale underwings. More uniform in winter. Short, dark bill with yellow base. Long, yellowish-green legs. — Slender and smaller than Redshank. Bobs with tail. **Vo:** Call a thin and clear 'tlu-ee', alarm call a Redshank-like, shrill, rapid 'chiff-chiff'. Song a melodic 'deedl-eedl-eedl' or 'leero-leero'. **Hab:** Mainly seen inland on marshes with scrubs and ponds. Coastal during migration. **Dist/Rem:** First recorded in Iceland in 1959, since then seen frequently and locally, mainly in the Lake Mývatn area. First proved breeding in 1981. **I:** Flóastelkur.

Late winter:
1. *Dark bill.*
2. *Grey-brown upperparts, spotted with white.*
3. *Barred tail and white rump.*
4. *Olive-green legs.*

Redshank, adult, summer.

Wood Sandpiper, late winter (moulting).

Dunlin
Calidris alpina
28

Adult, summer:
1. *Black bill, fairly decurved at tip.*
2. *Black patch on lower breast down to belly.*
3. *Black legs.*

16–20 cm — Breeder/Passage migrant — Sexes identical — 2

Stubby sandpiper of wetland and mudflats. In *summer* chestnut crown and upperparts, streaked black and fringed white. Pale supercilium. Upper breast pale with dark streaks. Black patch on lower breast down to belly. Thin, white wing-bar. White sides on dark-centered rump and tail. Black, fairly long bill, slightly decurved at tip. Dark-brown eyes. Rather short, black legs. *Winter* plumage lacks the black patch; brownish-grey above, fringed with white. White below with finely grey-streaked breast. *Juv* darker than *ad* winter, more like *ad* summer above, except for brownish colour instead of chestnut. Breast and flanks streaked and spotted with black. — Gregarious outside breeding grounds, often mixes with other waders. Flight fast, birds alternately showing dark and pale upper- and underparts. Stands rather hunched. Walks delicately. **Vo:** Call a whistled, nasal 'chrrrip', flock call a high-pitched 'beep' or 'trrrui'. Alarm call a 3-noted 'trrip'. Song a purring trill 'tritri ririri...', beginning with grunting 'rrhuee', singing in flight or on ground. **Hab:** Breeds in many kinds of wet- and dry land, e.g. wet meadows, higland moors, heathland etc. Probably most common as breeder on sedge marshes and wet, sandy grassland near coast. Outside breeding season and during migration prefers tidal mudflats and also inland in wetland areas. **Bre:** Nest is a scrape made in vegetation, lined with grass and moss, usually well hidden. Four eggs, laid late May to July, mainly in earlier half of June. **Dist:** Common and widespread in suitable habitats. Greenlandic Dunlins stage in Iceland during spring and late

Winter and juvenile plumage:
Lacks the black patch. Streaked
breast (more prominent on juv), white
belly and grey-brown above.

Summer.

summer. Main wintering grounds for Icelandic birds are in W-Africa. Usually a few sightings in winter on the SW shores. **Rem:** Little data available on breeding density, 20-40 pairs/sq. km probably common in lowlands but can reach 100 pairs in most suitable areas. More scattered in highland areas. The Icelandic name for Dunlin, *lóuþræll,* "Plover's slave," refers to frequent close association of Golden Plovers and Dunlins observed during breeding season. **I:** Lóuþræll.

Winter.

Dunlin, adult, summer.

Dunlin, juvenile.

Purple Sandpiper
Calidris maritima

29

Summer:
1. *Dark bill, yellow at base.*
2. *White, spotted dark belly, flanks and underwings.*
3. *Rufous and whitish-fringed above. Shows narrow white wing-bars in flight.*

20–22 cm — Breeder/Passage migrant/Winter visitor — Sexes similar — 2

A stocky sandpiper, in *summer* greyish-brown on head, neck and breast with blackish streaks and spots on throat, breast and flanks. White belly. Rufous and whitish-fringed above. In flight narrow, pale wing-bars and edges on secondaries and white rump with black centre-stripe. Darker in *winter*, uniform slate-grey on head, breast and upperparts contrasting with white belly. Whitish fringes on wings. Lower breast and flanks mottled. *Juv* coloured somewhere between summer and winter plumages. Slightly decurved dark bill, yellow at base. Dark-brown eyes. Short, yellowish legs, darker in summer. — Darkest of the small sandpipers, slightly larger and stockier than Dunlin. Flight low and direct, swims easily. Gregarious outside breeding season, form large flocks, sometimes mixed with other waders. Birds in flight show alternately dark and pale, upper- and underparts. Tame and easy to observe. **Vo:** Call a loud 'kuit' and lower 'kwit-it'. Alarm call a high-pitched trilling 'triitt-triitt'. During display flight a short, rapid trill 'pupupu...'. **Hab:** Breeds inland and on coast, inland habitats include barren mountains, lichen tundra, gravel flats, frequently close to water, on lowlands found on gravel flats and coastal heathlands. Outside breeding season mainly rocky shores, also tidal mudflats in late winter and spring. **Bre:** Nest is a shallow scrape, sparsely lined, often in moss or lichens, close to a stone or tuft of grass, with little cover. Clutch is 4 eggs, laid late May onwards, later in the highlands. Female leaves brood soon after

Winter:
1. *Slate grey head, back and breast.*
2. *White below.*
3. *Yellow legs.*

Winter.

hatching and young are tended by male. **Dist:** Fairly common and widespread breeder in suitable habitat. The most common wader in winter and the only one seen regularly on the north and east coast. Passage migrants from Greenland and Arctic Canada occur and some probably winter. Partly migratory. **I:** Sendlingur.

Purple Sandpiper in summer.

Purple Sandpiper in winter.

Sanderling
Calidris alba

30

20–21 cm — Passage migrant — Sexes similar — 2

A Dunlin-like wader. In *summer* rufous head, neck and breast, spotted with black. Dark above, fringed with rufous (♂) or grey (♀). Wing coverts grey. Pure white belly and vent. *Winter* plumage very pale; white head with grey crown and white underparts, grey upperparts. Broad, white wing-bar and dark bend of wing conspicuous in flight; white-edged dark tail and rump. *Juv* has blackish streaked crown, buffish head and breast and chequred white on black above. Short and straight, black bill. Dark-brown eyes. Black legs. — Bit larger and plumper than Dunlin, paler in *winter* and *juv* plumage. Extremely active, runs to and from waves on sandy shores. Gregarious. **Vo:** Call a high, short 'klit' and 'quit'. **Hab:** Mainly seen on sandy shores but also on tidal mudflats. **Dist:** Passage migrant. Sanderlings from Greenland and Arctic Canada stage in Iceland on their way to

Summer:
1. *Black, short and straight bill.*
2. *Rufous head, breast and back.*
3. *Black legs.*

Winter.

Winter (juvenile):
1. *Pale, darker above.*
2. *Conspicuous wing-bars, blackish shoulder-patch.*

and from the wintering grounds in the Old World. Some thousands arrive on west coast in May and from mid-July to mid-September. Very rare in summer and winter. **I:** Sanderla.

Sanderling, adult, summer.

Sanderling, juvenile.

Knot

Calidris canutus

31

23–25 cm — Passage migrant/Winter and summer visitor —
Sexes similar — 3

A stocky wader with short bill, neck and legs. In *summer* mostly
chestnut on head, neck, breast and belly. Blackish above with
chestnut fringes and crown streaked blackish. In *winter* mainly
grey above with thin white fringes resembling scales. Whitish
below with some streaks on more grey breast. *Juv* resembles *ad*
in winter plumage, but darker grey upperparts have more
distinct scaly pattern on breast fringed with buff. In *all plumages*
has greyish wings with white wing-bars, pale grey vermiculated
rump and grey tail. Black bill. Dark eyes. Greenish legs. —
Resembles Dunlin but much bigger, behaviour similar but
slower and flight stronger. Gregarious and form huge flocks

Summer:
In summer plumage chestnut on head,
neck, breast and belly. Wings grey.
Migrate in large flocks.

Winter.

Winter (juvenile):
1. Stocky and grey.
2. Short, thick and black bill.
3. White-fringed above, scaly
   appearance.
4. Short, pale-greenish legs.

(thousands). **Vo:** Call a hoarse 'knut', flight call a higher, whistling
'kwit-wit'. **Hab:** Breeds in High Arctic tundra. On passage prefers
tidal mudflats and rocky shores. Scarce inland. Wintering birds
seen with other waders, e.g. Oystercatcher, Turnstone and
Purple Sandpiper. **Dist:** Knots from Greenland and Arctic
Canada stage in Iceland on their way to and from the wintering
grounds in W-Europe. Most common on SW, W, NW and NE
shores. Some non-breeders stay all summer and a few dozen
winter in SW-Iceland. **Rem:** Spring passage is in May
(supposedly exceeding 200,000 birds), autumn passage is more
evenly spread, from mid-July to mid-September, with peaks at
end of July (*ads*) and in the last week of August (*juvs*). **I:**
Rauðbrystingur.

Knots in summer, flock in May.

Knot, juvenile.

Turnstone
Arenaria interpres

32

22–24 cm — Passage migrant/Winter and summer visitor —
Sexes similar — 2

Unmistakable, colourful wader. In *summer* black breast and
throat, black extending to eyes and nape of white head.
Streaked crown. Red-brown and black mantle and scapulars.
White underparts. In flight white back and wing-bars
conspicuous together with white and black on tail and rump and
white on wing-coverts. Duller in *winter* plumage, blackish-
brown or grey above and on head and breast, white throat. *Juv*
similar, but browner and more scaly above, plumage looks
"cleaner". Short, pointed black bill. Black eyes. Short, orange
legs. — Gregarious, but does not form larger flocks than a few
hundred. Forages in tidal zone, turning over small stones and
seaweed in search of food. Often seen with other waders, e.g.
Oystercatcher and Purple Sandpiper. **Vo:** Call a high chuckling,

Summer:
1. *Black breast. Black bands on white head and neck.*
2. *Red-brown above, pied with black and white.*

Summer.

Winter (juvenile):
1. *Sooty-brown on head, back and breast.*
2. *Orange legs.*

stacatto 'kree-re-rerere...', like ringing bells. Alarm call a short
'tuk-e-tuk-tuk'. **Hab:** Rocky shores and open beaches with rich
driftline of rotting seaweed, also mudflats. Few seen inland in
spring. **Dist:** Birds from Greenland and NE-Canada, wintering
mainly in W-Europe, stage in Iceland in spring and autumn,
especially on the western coasts. Some hundreds winter on SW
shores and non-breeders stay all summer. **I:** Tildra.

Turnstone, adult, summer.

Turnstone, juvenile.

Lapwing
Vanellus vanellus

33

28–31 cm — Vagrant/Irregular breeder — Sexes similar — 3

Best identified by long, wispy crest, looks black and white at a distance. In flight broad, rounded wings are distinctive. Dark above with greenish sheen. White from belly and lower breast out to underwing coverts. White cheeks. White wingtips. White tail with black terminal band. Chestnut undertail coverts. In *summer* black face, throat and breast. In *winter* face less black, throat and foreneck white. *Juv* duller, with pale fringes above and short crest. Short, black bill. Black eyes. Rufous legs. — Usually seen single or in small flocks. Erratic and tumbling flight with leisurely flapping wing-beats. **Vo:** Very variable, flight call is 'pee-wit'. **Hab:** Breeds in open, sparsely vegetated wetlands near farms. Winter vagrants mainly seen on shores and farmland. **Bre:** Nest is scrape in vegetation, no cover. Four eggs, laid in June. **Dist/Rem:** Annual vagrant, mainly seen September to May. Invasions during winter coincide with cold weather in Europe. Ten records of breeding known for the period 1959–88. **I:** Vepja.

Summer:
1. *Long, upcurved crest.*
2. *Black, green-glossed back and upperwings.*
3. *Black breast.*
4. *Broad, rounded wings.*

Grey Heron
Ardea cinerea

34

90–98 cm — Vagrant/Winter visitor — Sexes identical — 7

A very tall, grey wading bird. *Ad* is blue-grey above contrasting with paler head and neck to belly. Blue-grey upperwing coverts, dark flight feathers. Black streaks from eyes to tip of long crest. Black streaks on foreneck, flanks and belly. *Imm* has greyer head and neck, lacks prominent crest and is less streaked on neck and underparts. Yellow (*ad*) or brownish (*imm*), long, dagger-shaped bill. Long, brown to red (*ad*) or greyish (*imm*) legs, extending much beyond tail in flight. — Flies with slow, deep wing-beats and keeps long neck retracted and S-shaped. Stands motionless near water waiting for prey, either with neck erect or head sunk between shoulders. **Vo:** A deep harsh 'fraruk/harrk' in flight. **Hab:** Seashores, also streams, ponds and lakes with fish. **Dist:** Arrives in September (August), observed all over the country. In winter mainly in South and Southwestern parts of the country, single or in small flocks. Leaves in April (to June). Most are immatures and recoveries show they originate from Norway. **I:** Gráhegri.

Adult:
1. *Long and dagger-shaped, yellow bill.*
2. *Long neck, forms S in flight.*
3. *Long, wispy crest.*
4. *Brownish, long legs, extending beyond tail in flight.*

Lapwing, adult, summer.

Grey Heron, adult.

Red-necked Phalarope
Phalaropus lobatus   35

18–19 cm — Breeder — Sexes dissimilar, ♂ smaller, ♀ more colourful — 1

Small aquatic wader, with grey crown and hindneck down to mantle and breast. White throat. Orange-red neck-band stretches up to nape. Dark above with 2 pairs of buffish longitudinal stripes. White below. Distinct white wing-bars. In *winter* pale blue-grey above, white below with dark eye-stripe. *Juv* similar but darker, with grey crown, neck, breast and flanks and upperparts similar to *ad* summer. Thin, black bill. Dark eyes. Slate-grey legs. — Almost always seen swimming; spins in circles when feeding and dips bill quickly into water to catch insects and other invertebrates. Smaller than Grey Phalarope. Tame and easy to observe. **Vo:/Hab:** Wetlands, both in lowland areas and highlands, concentration found in rich wetland areas like the Lake Mývatn area. Outside breeding season mainly coastal or on brackish pools and ponds. Pelagic in winter. **Bre:** Nest is a depression in tussock, moss or dry grass, lined with grass and well covered. Four eggs are laid late May to late June. The male incubates and tends the young, sometimes polyandrous. **Dist:** Common, with concentrations in suitable habitats. Winters in western South-Atlantic. Recorded breeding density in suitable habitat is 15–30 "pairs"/sq.km. **I:** Óðinshani.

Summer:
1. *Thin, black bill.*
2. *Orange-red neck-collar.*
3. *White throat.*
4. *White wing-bars, distinctive in flight.*

Immature, and in winter.

Grey Phalarope
Phalaropus fulicarius   36

20–22 cm — Breeder — Sexes dissimilar, ♂ smaller, ♀ more colourful — 2

Female summer:
1. *Thick, black tipped, yellow bill.*
2. *Rufous neck and underparts.*
3. *White cheeks.*
4. *Buff streaked mantle.*

♀ in *summer* has dark crown, chin and base of bill, white cheeks. Rufous neck and underparts. Streaked buff mantle. White wing-bars. ♂ is duller, with streaked crown and often some white on belly. Yellow bill with black tip. In *winter* resembles Red-necked Phalarope, but slightly larger and stockier with stouter and broader, black bill, heavier head and thicker neck. Also paler and less streaked above. *Juv* similar, but darker above. Dark-brown eyes. Greyish legs with yellow lobes. — Behaviour similar to Red-necked Phalarope. **Vo:** Shrill 'twit' or 'prip', softer 'dreeet'. **Hab:** In summer especially coastal lagoons and pools, shores with rich driftline of rotting seaweed, also sandy areas near coast, grown with moss and sedges with pools and streamlets. Oceanic outside breeding season. **Bre:** Nest is scrape hidden in vegetation. Four eggs, laid in June and incubated by male. Often polyandrous. **Dist:** Rare, found in scattered, small colonies. **Rem:** A census in 1987 recorded only 40–50 "pairs". Remains only 1–2 months on breeding grounds, arriving in late May, and most have left by late July. Few are observed until October, these probably include passage migrants from High Arctic breeding grounds. **I:** Þórshani.

Red-necked Phalarope, female, in summer.

Grey Phalarope, female in summer.

Coot
Fulica atra

37

36–38 cm — Vagrant/Irregular breeder — Sexes identical — 4

A waterbird, with large body, and small head and tail. Slaty-black body and black, glossy head. White rear edge of wing seen in flight. *First year* birds are duller. White bill and frontal shield. Red eyes. Green-grey legs. Large feet with long, lobed toes, projecting behind tail or almost drooping in flight. — Swims high, with nodding head movements and dives with a plunge. Runs across water before taking off and flies laboriously. Walks easily. Unshy and frequently associates with ducks. **Vo:** Calls variable, typical is a loud, short 'tewk' or a piping 'howk'. **Hab:** In winter on ice-free lakes, ponds and slow rivers, also on sheltered coastal bays. In summer exclusively on freshwater. **Bre:** A floating nest made of vegetation, built in sedges etc. Eggs 5–12. **Dist/Rem:** Observed in all seasons, mainly single birds; most records stem from November-December. Observed in all parts of the country, most from the southwest and northeast. Some breeding attempts are known in Iceland. **I:** Bleshæna.

Adult:
1. *White bill and frontal shield.*
2. *Green-grey legs. Long, lobed toes.*
3. *Tail inconspicuous. Legs extend considerably beyond it or droop in flight.*
4. *Mainly slate-black.*

Water Rail
Rallus aquaticus

38

23–28 cm — Vagrant/Formerly breeder — Sexes identical — 3

A skulking, compact wetland bird. Brown above, streaked with black. Dark blue-grey from head down to belly. Flanks barred black and white. Short tail often held cocked, showing white undertail coverts. Wings short and rounded. *Imm* with white throat and paler face, mottled brown on neck and below. Long, reddish bill. Red eyes. Pale-brown legs, long toes. — Solitary, crepuscular and secretive. More often heard than seen (on breeding grounds) or footprints found (in winter). Flies rarely; flutters with long legs dangling. Swims short distances. **Vo:** Call a hard, drawn-out 'gep-gep-gep'; a variety of purring, grunting, groaning and squealing notes, especially a "wild, pig-like" scream. **Hab:** Wetlands with dense vegetation, e.g. sedge bogs, marshes and fens. In winter open springs, creeks, ditches and hot-spring areas. **Bre:** Nest is built in sedge tussocks, often over shallow water and well hidden. Eggs 7–12, laid in June-July. **Dist/Rem:** Formerly an uncommon breeder in lowland sedge marshes, mainly in the south. Has not been found breeding for more than 30 years. Birds observed in winter and autumn are thought to be vagrants. Habitat destruction (drainage) is claimed to be main reason for decline. **I:** Keldusvín.

Adult:
1. *Long, reddish bill.*
2. *Brownish legs with long toes, dangling in flight.*
3. *Short, cocked tail.*
4. *Brown above, slate-grey below.*

Coot, adult.

Water Rail, adult.

Gulls, Terns and Skuas

The upper mandible of the long and powerful beak of most gull species is hooked at the tip, while the lower carries a downward projection near the front which is coloured red in several species. Their wings are long and powerful, and though these birds frequently glide along at ease, they occasionally show spurts of great speed and agility. Gulls feed by diving a short distance into the sea and grabbing their food. They also scavenge on beaches and are greatly attracted by organic waste. The smaller gulls, the Black-headed Gull, Common Gull and the Lesser Black-backed Gull, live almost entirely on insects and other small creatures during the summer. In their breding haunts it is common to find regurgitated pellets consisting of indigestible parts of the prey; birds of prey do the same thing. All gulls have webbing between their front toes, but the rear toe is without webbing, small and weak or totally absent.

The Arctic Skua and Great Skua are basically dark brown in colour. While they are related to gulls, which they resemble, they constitute a separate family, the Stercorariidae. The central feathers of the tail are longer than the others. Both species rob other birds of their food.

The Arctic Tern and Black Tern are closely related to the gulls and constitute a subfamily, the Sterninae. Most terns are rather small with long wings and are therefore capable of great agility in flight. They nest in dense colonies. Terns catch their food near the surface of the water and will also take insects in flight.

Gulls' colouring and plumage changes often make identification difficult, and as they are extremely common it is appropriate to give a clear account of the different features of each species.

Gulls change part of their plumage during their first autumn. They shed most of their head and body plumage. Thereafter, they moult twice a year: in autumn (August–October), when they shed all feathers, and late winter (February–April) when they shed their head and body plumage.

The large gulls, the Great and Lesser Black-backed Gull, the Herring Gull, the Glaucous Gull and the Iceland Gull acquire adult plumage in their fourth winter. Young gulls in their first year of life are for the most part covered with dark spots. The young of the Great Black-backed Gull is white on the head, neck and underparts, with a speckled back and wings, except for the primaries and secondaries, which are dark brown. The rump and tail are light-coloured, except for a broad brown-black band across the end of the tail feathers. The Lesser Black-backed Gull and the Herring Gull have the same tail colouring, but are otherwise speckled with dark brown spots. These two species resemble each other closely, but the Herring Gull is lighter in colour. The primaries of both are dark brown, except for primaries nos. 5–10 of the Herring Gull, which are light-coloured and form a sort of speculum. This is the most conspicuous characteristic distinguishing the young of these species. During the birds' second winter, the lighter parts of the plumage become paler and in time the speckled back and wing feathers take on the colouring of the adult bird. In their third winter of life they resemble the adult birds fairly closely, with the dark band on the tail becoming lighter and finally disappearing, while the beak and eyes become lighter in colour.

In Iceland, where the distribution areas of the Herring Gull and the Glaucous Gull overlap in the north and west of the country, the two species have interbred. Most of the specimens of both stocks show signs of this crossing, though it is more evident in the Herring Gulls. Naturally, this crossing makes identification even more difficult.

The young of the Glaucous Gull and the Iceland Gull have speckled light brown plumage and lack the dark band on the tail which characterizes the young of the other large gull species. In their second winter they become paler, often becoming almost white, but in their third winter their backs begin to turn grey.

The Common Gull in its first winter of life is rather similar to the Herring Gull in its second. The back is grey, but the breast and underparts are pale with brown flecks. The wings are speckled with dark colouring, while the rump and tail are white with a dark band. During the summer these gulls grow paler and by their second winter they resemble the adult bird, acquiring the full adult plumage in their third winter.

In the winters, the adults of all these gull species develop brown speckles on their heads.

The young of the Kittiwake acquire the plumage of the mature adult in their third winter. During their first winter, Kittiwakes have clearly defined black stripes on their necks, wings and tail-ends, otherwise being coloured grey and white. Mature Kittiwakes acquire dark patches on their ear-coverts and the back of their necks in the winter.

The Ivory Gull and the Black-headed Gull take on the plumage of the adult in their second winter. Black-headed Gulls which have just learned to fly are speckled with dark colouring on the upper parts of their bodies, but grow paler as the summer progresses. The Black-headed Gull loses its black hood in the winter, taking on dark patches on the nape and ear-coverts.

Great Black-backed Gull

Larus marinus

39

Adult, summer:
1. *Yellow bill. Red spot on gonys.*
2. *Black mantle and upperwings.*
3. *Pale-pinkish.*
4. *White spotted, black wing tips.*

64–78 cm — Breeder — Sexes similar — 7

The largest Icelandic gull. *Ad* in *summer* plumage has a uniform black mantle, back and upperwings, same colour on white-spotted wing tips. Other feathered parts pure white, except dusky, black-tipped underwings. Long, yellow bill with red spot on lower mandible. Eyes yellow with red orbital ring. Pale-pinkish legs. In *winter* head and neck mottled pale-brown. *Juv/1st winter* has dark-brown mantle and upperwings, chequered paler, except blackish-brown flight feathers. From head down to belly pale, with some brownish streaks, more conspicuous on *juv.* Whitish rump and base of tail, with broad, not clearly defined brownish-black tail band. Dark bill and eyes. In *2nd* and *3rd winter* the pale parts gradually become whiter and mantle and upperwings blacker, tail band disappears and bill and eyes become paler; bill yellowish with dark band near tip. Acquires *ad* plumage in fourth winter. These plumage changes are typical for large gulls. — Much larger than Lesser Black-backed Gull, with relatively shorter, broader wings and shorter legs, more powerful bill. Flies with slow strong wing-beats. **Vo:** Calls are deep and low-pitched 'klaow', barking 'ga-ga-ga...' or 'gowk' etc. **Hab:** Breeds in all kinds of coastal habitats, e.g. fluvial plains, mountains, islands and skerries, also inland on islands in lakes and rivers, in highland oases or even on nunataks. In winter

Second summer.

First winter, immature:
1. *Head, breast and belly whitish with some streaks.*
2. *Mottled mantle and upperwings, blackish-brown flight feathers.*
3. *Whitish rump and tail. Broad, dark tail band.*

mainly coastal, often near urban areas, also at open lakes and rivers. **Bre:** Bulky nest made of sticks, seaweed, grass and heather, built on ground or on top of stacks or broad cliff ledges. Clutch of 3 eggs laid end of April to end of May. **Dist:** The most common and widely distributed of the large gulls in Iceland, found breeding single or in colonies. Mostly sedentary, but some *imms* winter in the Faroes and the British Isles. **Rem:** This graceful bird is unpopular among Eider farmers and others, because of its predatory habits and is proscribed all year. It is omnivorous but eats mainly fish, marine and coastal invertebrates, fish offal and other refuse. **I:** Veiðibjalla, svartbakur.

Great Black-backed Gull, adult, summer.

Great Black-backed Gull, first winter immatures.

Lesser Black-backed Gull

Larus fuscus

40

52–67 cm — Breeder — Sexes similar — 5

The characteristic large gull seen inland in S- and SW-Iceland during summer. *Ad summer* has slate-grey back and upperwings and white tips to black primaries; two outermost primaries also with white spots near tip. Other feathered parts pure white. Yellow bill with red spot near gonys. Pale-yellow eyes, red orbital ring. Yellow legs. Head and underparts of *juv* rather uniformly streaked dark grey-brown. Dark-brown and scaly upperparts. Almost uniformly brownish-black flight feathers and greater coverts, no pale patch ("window") on inner primaries; compare with Herring Gull. Pale rump and tail contrasting with dark tail-band. Black bill. Flesh-coloured legs. Sequence of plumage changes in *2nd* and *3rd year* similar to Great Black-backed Gull. — Told from Great Black-backed Gull by smaller size, colour of back, thinner bill and slightly narrower and more pointed wings, projecting more beyond tail when folded. Swims buoyantly. Gregarious, not as shy as Great Black-backed Gull, more restricted to inhabited areas. **Vo:** Alarm call 'gag-gag-gag'. Call a

Adult, summer:
1. Back and upperwings slate-grey.
2. Clear-cut black wing tips with white spots, darker than back and upperwings.
3. Yellow legs.

Note: Smaller, more delicate and with relatively longer wings than Great Black-backed Gull.

2nd summer moulting to 3rd winter.

Juvenile:
1. Body and wings streaked dark-brown.
2. Pale rump and tail, black tail-band.
3. Dark inner primaries, without a pale patch.
4. Flesh-coloured legs.

repeated, loud and yelping 'kyow'. Noisy in breeding grounds. Voice is higher than of Great Black-backed Gull, but deeper and more nasal than Herring Gull. **Hab:** Breeds on gravel flats and heaths, mainly on coast but also inland, sometimes in association with Great Black-backed Gull. Outside breeding season mainly seen on coast and in urban areas and farmland. **Bre:** Nests on ground often besides or between stones and tussocks. Nest is made of moss and grass or other vegetation, lined with feathers. Clutch of 3 eggs laid late May to early June. **Dist:** Common, breeding in colonies in the south and southwest, less common elsewhere but increasing. Migrant; wintering grounds are probably in Iberia and NW-Africa. Very rare in winter. **Rem:** First recorded breeding in the 1920's. The Icelandic population belongs to the British and W-European subspecies *L.f. graellsii*. Forages more on insects than other large gulls in Iceland. **I:** Sílamáfur.

Lesser Black-backed Gull, adult, summer.

Lesser Black-backed Gull, juvenile.

Herring Gull
Larus argentatus

41

55–67 cm — Breeder — Sexes similar — 6

The largest gull with grey back and black wingtips. *Ad summer* has uniform, pale grey upperparts and wings with clear-cut black wingtips and white spots and two obvious "mirrors" on folded wings. Other feathered parts white. In *winter* dusky head and neck marks. Yellow bill with red spot on gonys. Pale yellow iris, red orbital ring. Pale-flesh legs. *Juv* very similar to Lesser Black-backed Gull, except for paler appearance, pale inner primaries forming a conspicuous pale patch ("window"), and paler, more fringed greater coverts lacking the uniform dark bar of Lesser Black-backed. In *2nd* year back and upperwings become greyer and underparts paler, but "window" remains on primaries (see drawing). Plumage changes follow same sequence as for Great Black-backed. — Heavily built, with proportionally short, broad wings. **Vo:** Similar to Lesser Black-backed Gull, but higher-pitched. Usual calls are 'kleow' and crowing 'klaow', also short 'ge-ge-ge'. **Hab:** Breeds near coast on grassy slopes, cliff ledges, islands, gravel flats and sand dunes, etc. Costal in winter. **Bre:** Nest a bulky structure made of dry grass, seaweed and sticks. Clutch of 2–3 eggs laid May to early

Adult, summer:
1. *Yellow bill with red spot on gonys.*
2. *Pale-grey back and upperwings.*
3. *Pale-flesh legs.*
4. *Black and white markings on wing tips.*

First winter, immature:
1. *Similar to Lesser Black-backed Gull, but has paler appearance.*
2. *Pale inner primaries, forming a "window" and paler, more fringed greater coverts. Also lesser contrasting grey rump.*

Second summer.

June. **Dist:** Breeds from the northeast coast clockwise to southwest. Partly migratory; mainly immatures migrate to British Isles in winter. **Rem:** Started breeding in 1920's after a large-scale invasion from NW-Europe. Has hybridized extensively with Glaucous Gull and hybrids are fertile. **I:** Silfurmáfur.

Herring Gull, adult, summer.

Herring Gull, first winter immature.

Common Gull

Larus canus **42**

40–42 cm — Breeder — Sexes similar — 4

Ad resembles small Herring Gull. Upperparts are pale grey and wing tips black with white spots. Other feathered parts white. Bill rather thin, almost without gonys and lacks red spot. Head streaked in *winter*. *Juv* largely greyish-brown, with blackish bill and flesh-brown legs. Black band on whitish tail. Brown back changes to blue-grey in first autumn. *1st winter* bird has whiter head and body, uniform grey mantle and scapulars and brown mottled upperwings with dark flight feathers. *1st summer* whiter head and body and paler wing-pattern. *2nd winter* is similar to *ad*, has lost black tail band, but primaries and primary coverts are darker. Bill has thin dark band near tip. — Larger than Black-headed Gull but smaller and lighter than Herring Gull with more rounded head. Flight buoyant. **Vo:** High and shrill 'klee-ya' or 'hieea', higher-pitched and weaker than Herring Gull, sometimes resembles a cat's miaow. **Hab:** Breeds in small colonies or with other gulls, especially Black-headed. Mostly near coast, but also inland, nesting on shingle banks along rivers, heaths, sand dunes etc. Winters on coasts near urban areas. **Bre:** Nests on ground among rocks and gravel or in vegetation. Nest is made of grass, moss and sedge. Clutch of 2–3 eggs laid May to June. **Dist:** Breeds in scattered localities around the country, most common in the north and southwest. Winters mainly in SW-Iceland. Ringing recoveries abroad from the Faroes and Scotland. **Rem:** Regular visitor before first suspected breeding attempt at Akureyri in 1936. First nest found in 1955 near Reykjavík. Since then breeding population has increased and is now estimated at c. 300 pairs. **I:** Stormmáfur.

Adult, summer:
1. *Yellow-green bill.*
2. *Pale-grey mantle and wings.*
3. *Black wing tips with white spots.*
4. *Greenish-yellow legs.*

First winter, immature:
1. *Mottled-brown head. Black-tipped bill.*
2. *Grey mantle, wing coverts mottled-brown, darker flight feathers.*
3. *White tail and rump, black tail-band.*
4. *Flesh-pinkish legs.*

Common Gull, adult, summer.

Common Gull, first winter immature.

Black-headed Gull

Larus ridibundus   43

Adult, summer:
1. Red bill.
2. Dark-brown hood.
3. Red legs.

34–37 cm — Breeder — Sexes similar — 4

The smallest breeding gull, a common wetland bird. *Ad summer*
has pale-grey upperparts, black primary tips on upperwings
and almost all black primaries on underwing, except for
outermost primaries which are white with black tips on both
sides. Dark-brown hood. In *winter* (August to March) head lacks
hood, with blackish ear marks. Red bill. Brown eyes with red
orbital ring and white eye-ring in summer. *Juv* is mottled-brown
on head and above, but becomes paler in autumn. In *1st winter*
plumage white on head, neck and underparts. Wing coverts
with dark bars and tips of flight feathers dark. Black tail-band.
Pinkish bill with black tip. Acquires *ad* plumage already in 2nd
autumn. — This small gull is unmistakable in all plumages,
lighter and smaller than Kittiwake and Common Gull, flight more
buoyant. Not as pelagic as Kittiwake. Gregarious and rather
tame. **Vo:** Noisy at breeding grounds, utters a screaming, harsh
'kwarr', 'krreeay', short 'kvuk' etc. **Hab:** Breeds in colonies in
different kinds of wet and dry habitats, inland and on coast, e.g.
deltas, marshes, bogs, sedge-bordered lakes or ponds, islands
in lakes or streams and even on shingle along rivers and coastal
heathland, often with Arctic Terns. Winters on coasts. **Bre:** Nest
on ground, often quite a bulky structure in wet areas. Clutch of
2–3 eggs laid late April to beginning of June. **Dist:** Main colonies
are in the central south, southwest and central north, but smaller
and more scattered colonies elsewhere. Wintering birds choose
towns and villages on southwest and north coast, but migrants
move mainly to W-Europe and also N-America. The main
colonies are in the central south, southwest and central north,
but smaller and more scattered colonies elsewhere. Wintering
birds found in harbours and at fish factories in southwest and
north; migrants move mainly to W-Europe, but also N-America.
Rem: A new immigrant, first nest recorded in 1911. The only gull
found in large numbers inland in summer, foraging much on
insects. **I:** Hettumáfur.

Immature, winter:
1. Black spots behind eye. Pink,
   black-tipped bill.
2. Mottled-brown above. Dark greater
   wing coverts and tips of flight
   feathers.
3. White tail with black terminal band.

Black-headed Gull, adult, summer.

Black-headed Gull, immature, winter.

Kittiwake
Rissa tridactyla

44

38–40 cm — Breeder — Sexes similar — 4

Common small gull of bird cliffs and open sea, the size of Common Gull. *Ad* has blue-grey back and upperwings, all black wingtips. Other feathered parts white. In *winter* nape and hindneck grey, blackish spots on ear-coverts. Yellow bill. Eyes black with red orbital ring. Short, black legs. *Juv* and *1st winter* birds have head like *ad* winter and black half-collar on hindneck. Back and lesser coverts as *ad*, dark diagonal band across wings, forming a "W". Inner primaries and secondaries white. Black band at end of slightly forked tail. By *1st summer* black colour of tail has faded, *2nd year* birds similar to *ads*. — Gregarious. Flight graceful with rapid beats. **Vo:** At breeding grounds a nasal, loud 'kitti-week', otherwise silent. **Hab:** More pelagic than other gulls, often seen far from land, commonly in wake of ships. Breeds on coastal cliffs, often in large colonies with other seabirds, also on top of rocky islands and skerries. **Bre:** Nest made of grass, moss and seaweed, cemented together and plastered on the rock with mud, excrement and saliva. Clutch of 2 eggs laid late May to early June. **Dist:** Abundant in colonies all along the coast. Small numbers winter inshore, but most are oceanic. Icelandic Kittiwakes have been recovered abroad in Greenland (mainly *juvs*), Newfoundland and in Europe from the Kola Peninsula south to Gibraltar. **Rem:** Increasing in last decades. Kittiwakes were formerly harvested for food, mainly eggs and young were taken. **I:** Rita.

Adult, summer:
1. *Yellow bill.*
2. *Black legs.*
3. *Blue-grey back.*
4. *Black wingtips without white spots.*

First winter:
1. *Dark bill. Black half-collar on hindneck.*
2. *Black band across upperwings, forming a W.*
3. *Narrow black tail band.*

Kittiwake, adult, summer.

Kittiwakes, adult, summer.

Kittiwake, first winter immature.

Glaucous Gull

Larus hyperboreus

45

Adult, summer:
1. *Yellow bill, red spot on gonys.*
2. *No black marks on body or wings.*
3. *Wings project only slightly beyond tail.*

62–68 cm — Breeder/Winter visitor — Sexes similar — 7

One of the characteristic large gulls in many coastal areas, mainly in winter. *Ad summer* has pale-grey mantle and upperwings and white wingtips; other parts are white. Head streaked in winter. Yellow bill with red spot on gonys. Pale-pinkish legs. Yellow eyes. *Juv/1st winter* mottled buffish-brown, darker above, without tail band. Pinkish, black-tipped bill. Pinkish legs and dark eyes. In *2nd year* paler and less barred, sometimes uniformly white, especially *2nd summer*. In *3rd year* similar to *ad*, except brownish areas on wings and tail, usually with dark ring near tip of yellowish bill. — A heavy gull, similar to Greater Black-backed Gull in behaviour and appearance. Very similar to Iceland Gull. Wings not projecting much beyond tail. **Vo:** Similar to Herring Gull, but shriller and more hoarse. **Hab:** Breeds on coasts in large colonies on vegetated cliffs in mountains and steep slopes, sometimes on top of stacks. Coastal and on open sea in winter. The most common large gull seen on the fishing banks. Sedentary population augmented by winter visitors from more northern regions. **Bre:** Nest made of moss,

First winter, immature:
1. *Mottled-brown all over.*
2. *Pink, black-tipped bill.*
3. *Tail without tail band.*

Moulting from 2nd summer
to 3rd winter.

grass and some feathers. Clutch of (2-)3 eggs laid in latter half of May. **Dist/Rem:** Main colonies found in Breiðafjörður and Vestfirðir in the west and northwest. Other colonies in the southwest and east now occupied by hybrids (Glaucous x Herring) and Herring Gull, but some few pure Glaucous are also found in these colonies. **I:** Hvítmáfur.

Glaucous Gull, adult, summer.

Glaucous Gull, first winter immature.

Iceland Gull

Larus glaucoides 46

52–60 cm — Winter visitor — Sexes similar — 5

Resembles Glaucous Gull but smaller and more delicate with rounded head and steeper forehead contrasting with flatter head of Glaucous. Plumage sequence of non-breeders similar to Glaucous Gull. Yellow bill with red spot (*ad*), much shorter and thinner than on Glaucous. *1st winter's* bill darker, with more black on tip. Pinkish-grey legs, shorter than on Glaucous. Reddish orbital ring in *summer*. — Wings project well beyond tail, narrower and longer than on Glaucous, so Iceland Gull appears lighter in flight. Swimming bird appears more buoyant than Glaucous Gull and resembles Fulmar in that respect. **Vo:** Like Glaucous Gull, higher-pitched than Herring Gull. **Hab:** Breeds on cliffs and rocky coasts. Coastal in Iceland and often mixes with other gulls. Rarely seen on shore, though sometimes on lakes and lagoons near sea. **Dist:** Winter visitor from Greenland and Arctic Canada. In Iceland from September to May (mainly October to April), often in large flocks. Sometimes seen in summer. **I:** Bjartmáfur.

Adult, summer:
1. *No black marks.*
2. *Pale-yellow, short, thin bill.*
3. *Long wings, giving flight a light appearance, and projected well beyond tail when folded.*

Second winter:
1. *Whitish body and wings with scattered brown spots.*
2. *Head delicate and more rounded than Glaucous Gull.*

Note:
First winter immature has similar plumage as same age Glaucous Gull.

Iceland Gull, adult, summer.

Iceland Gull, second winter immature.

Ivory Gull

Pagophila eburnea　　　　　　　　　　**47**

40–43 cm — Winter visitor — Sexes similar — 4

Ad all-white with dark-grey, yellow-tipped bill. Dark eyes, red orbital ring. Black legs. *Imm* with grey smudgy marks on lores and chin; black spots on upperparts (on primary coverts etc.). Primaries and tail feathers with black tips, forming a narrow band on tail . Greyish, yellow-tipped bill. Black eyes. Acquires *ad* plumage already in 1st summer. — Stocky and pigeon-like. Long, pointed wings, tern-like buoyant flight. Unwilling to swim. **Vo:** Tern-like calls. **Hab/Dist:** Breeds in High Arctic, on cliffs or ground. Annual winter visitor (October to May), mainly in North Iceland. Follows drift ice and when it reaches Icelandic waters, small flocks can be observed, otherwise usually seen single. **I:** Ísmáfur.

Immature:
1. *Mostly white.*
2. *Grey, yellow-tipped bill.*
3. *Narrow, black band on wings and tail edge.*
4. *Black legs in all plumages.*

Note:
Adult:
All-white, paler bill.

Black Tern

Chlidonias niger　　　　　　　　　　**48**

22–24 cm — Vagrant — Sexes similar — 3

Ad in summer blackish below except for white undertail coverts. Black head and neck. Grey wings, back and uppertail, underwings contrasting with underbody, females slightly duller. Tail deeply forked. Black bill. Red-brown legs. Winter, *juv* and *imm* plumages have black cap and mark on side of neck, white face, neck and underparts, grey upperparts. Mantle and upperwings darker on *juv*. — Flies to and fro over water, dipping to surface to snatch insects, does not plunge or dive like Arctic Tern. **Vo:** Rather silent. Higher pitched and more squeaky than Arctic Tern. **Hab/Bre:** Nests usually in colonies in fens, marshes or in shallows of ponds, laying 2–3 eggs in a heap of vegetation, nest often floating. Coastal in passage. **Dist/Rem:** Summer migrant, recorded from May to October, mainly June and July. Recorded in all parts of the country, most often at coastal lagoons or near coast, but also at inland lakes and ponds, mostly singles. Birds identified both to the N-American race (*C. n. surinamensis*) and the European race (*C. n. niger*) have been observed. Failed breeding attempts in 1983 and 1984 were recorded in a ternery at Stokkseyri, S-Iceland. **I:** Kolþerna.

Adult, summer:
1. *Black bill.*
2. *Black head, neck and underparts.*
3. *Dark-grey wings.*
4. *White undertail.*

Ivory Gull, immature, in autumn.

Black Tern, adult, summer.

Arctic Tern

Sterna paradisaea

33–35 — Breeder — Sexes identical — 4

The only abundant tern in Iceland. *Ad* in summer has a black cap from base of bill back to nape. Body mainly blue-grey, except for whitish line beneath cap, white tail coverts and hind belly, darker above. Black-tipped primaries (narrow black trailing edge). Red bill and short red legs. Dark-brown eyes. First summer (and winter plumage) has white forehead, breast and belly, with dark-grey bend of wing and shorter tail streamers. Black bill and legs. *Juv* has white forehead and fringed brown and grey mantle and upperwings, slightly forked tail. Black bill. Red legs. Second summer similar to adult. — Slender with pointed, long and narrow wings and deeply forked tail. Flight buoyant. Usually hovers and plunges for food. Poor walker. **Vo:** Noisy, especially in colonies. Song a squeaky 'pee-pee' or 'pree-e', also 'kee-yah'. Alarm call 'kree-err-kirri'. **Hab:** Variable during summer, largest colonies are on low-lying coastal areas and on offshore islands. Also found inland at lakes and rivers, even in the central highlands and islets in ponds in towns (e.g. Lake Tjörnin in Reykjavík). Frequently shares breeding habitat with Black-headed Gull and waterfowl. Coastal outside breeding season. **Bre:** Breeds single or in colonies of varying size. Nest scrape made in ground, sometimes lined with pebbles or vegetation. Clutch of 1–3 eggs, normally 2, laid from late May onwards, most birds lay in early June. **Dist:** Widely distributed in Iceland. Winters in S-Atlantic (off SW-Africa) or Antarctic waters. Birds from northern areas are possibly transmigrants in Iceland. **Rem:** The Arctic Tern is very aggressive on the breeding grounds and offers good protection to Eiders and other waterfowl nesting close by. — First summer terns begin to show up in colonies in early June, with main influx in late June and in July. — The largest colonies have been estimated to number more than 10,000 pairs. **I:** Kría.

1. *Red bill.*
2. *Black cap.*
3. *Short, red legs.*
4. *Deeply forked tail. Long, pointed wings.*

Winter/immature.

Arctic Tern, adult, summer.

Arctic Tern, adult, summer, hovering.

✓

Arctic Skua
Stercorarius parasiticus   **50**

1. *Black bill.*
2. *Central tail feathers pointed and elongated, projecting 5–10 cm.*

41–46 cm — Breeder — Sexes similar — 5

Common skua of coastal areas and inland marshes and heaths. *Ad* is mainly dark-brown, blackish on crown, wings and tail. Outermost primaries white-shafted, more obvious from below. Central tail feathers pointed, elongated, projecting 5–10 cm. Light phase birds (increasing to north, 10–40% of population) are pale on cheeks, neck, breast and belly, often with dark breast band. Intermediates occur. Black bill and legs. Dark-brown eyes. *Juv* variable, usually barred brown and with shorter central tail feathers. — Flight graceful and buoyant. — **Vo:** Usual calls nasal mew 'eh-glaw...' or 'kay-yow'. **Hab:** Breeds in a wide range of habitats from coast up to 700 m a.s.l., e.g. marshes and heathland. Also in Central Highland oases and even nunataks. Can form loose colonies on sandy coastal flats. Pelagic outside breeding season. **Bre:** Nest a scrape made in vegetation. Clutch of 2 eggs is laid from end of May to beginning of June. **Dist:** Breeds in suitable habitats all over the country. Winters in Southern Hemisphere. **Rem:** Renowned for its ability to steal food from other birds, main victims are Arctic Tern, Puffin, Kittiwake and Fulmar. **I:** Kjói.

Long-tailed Skua
Stercorarius longicaudus   **51**

46–51 cm — Passage migrant — Sexes similar — 5

Central tail feathers (13–25 cm) longer, narrower and more flexible than on Arctic Skua, also paler neck, underparts and underwings, otherwise resembles light phase Arctic Skua. Annual passage migrant en route to and from breeding grounds in the Arctic. **I:** Fjallkjói.

Light phase:
1. *Black cap.*
2. *Pale neck and underparts.*
3. *Light patches at base of primaries (both phases).*
4. *Black legs.*

Pomarine Skua
Stercorarius pomarinus   **52**

46–51 cm — Passage migrant — Sexes similar — 5

Central tail feathers (5–10 cm) twisted, with rounded and broad ends. Larger and stouter than Arctic Skua, but plumage similar. Dark and light phases, dark more common. Passage pattern similar to Long-tailed Skua. Pomarine more pelagic than Long-tailed which is more often seen inland **I:** Ískjói.

Long-tailed Skua.

Pomarine Skua, light phase.

Arctic Skuas, dark phase (left) and intermediate (right).

Arctic Skua, light phase.

Great Skua

Stercorarius skua

53–58 cm — Breeder — Sexes similar — 6

Heavy-bodied, short-necked skua, resembling a large, dark gull, the characteristic bird of fluvio-glacial flats in the south and southeast. Dark brown with lighter feathers on head, neck, breast and back. Inner half of primaries white, wing forming distinguishing patches seen on flying birds. Wings broad and rounded. Tail short and rounded with central feathers slightly projecting. Black, large bill with hooked tip. Black eyes. Black, sturdy legs. *Juv* similar to *ad* but darker. — Much heavier than other skuas with broader wings. **Vo:** At breeding grounds, when aggressive near nest, a deep 'tuk-tuk' or gruff 'hak-ak-ak'; flight call 'sheerr' or 'a-er'. **Hab:** Breeds in scattered colonies on fluvial flats near coast, also on capes and even in highland oases. Oceanic in winter. **Bre:** Clutch of 2 eggs laid in 2nd half of May. Nest a scrape, often without any nesting material. **Dist:** Scattered to common on breeding grounds, the largest colonies are on the south coast. Winters in the North Atlantic. **Rem:** Thirty years ago c. 80% of the N-Atlantic population bred in Iceland. Due to increase in other parts of the range this is down to c. 50% now. The Great Skua is known to pursue and steal food from other seabirds, including gulls, alcids and even Gannet, and forces them to drop their prey or disgorge it. Also catches fish and birds, and follows fishing boats and trawlers. Very aggressive on breeding grounds, attacking people approaching the nest. **I:** Skúmur.

1. *Black, hook-tipped bill.*
2. *Black, sturdy legs.*
3. *White patches at base of primaries.*
4. *Large, dark-brown and stout build. Short, rounded tail.*

Great Skua, adult.

Great Skuas, adults.

Pigeons and Doves

Pigeons and doves are stoutly-built birds with small heads and dense, soft plumage. Their beaks are hard at the front but soft further back, and there is a cere (a thick patch of skin) at the base of the beak. They live on seeds, berries, buds and invertebrates. When doves and pigeons drink, they put their beaks below the surface of the water and suck, as they are able to close their nostrils. Their throats swell out when they coo. Sharp flapping noises are also heard from the wings, which strike together in flight, both when the birds fly in panic and during courtship flights. The chicks are born blind and practically bare, and during their first days they live on crop-milk produced by the mucous membrane of the crop.

Pigeons and doves are gregarious birds which have settled in many parts of the world, with the exception of the polar regions. Only one species is naturalized in urban areas in Iceland: the domesticated variety of the Rock Dove, known as the Feral Pigeon. Three other species have been sighted in Iceland: the Wood Pigeon, the Turtle Dove and the Collared Dove. They are vagrants from the European mainland. The Wood Pigeon and the Collared Dove have nested and raised young in Iceland.

Feral Pigeon
Columba livia   54

Adult Rock Dove type:
1. *Main colour grey-blue. Glossy, purple-green neck-sides.*
2. *White upper-rump.*
3. *Two black wing-bars.*

31–34 cm — Breeder (introduced) — Sexes identical — 4

The Feral or Domestic Pigeon is descended from the Rock Dove, a native bird of Europe including the Faroes. General colour of the Rock Dove is blue-grey. Glossy purple-green on neck sides. Whitish upper rump and underwings. Two black wing-bars. Tail grey with black tail-band. Grey to black bill with white cere. Orange eyes. Pink legs. *Juv* plumage is browner, no gloss on neck, darker underwings. — Feral pigeons often show their ancestral markings (c.f. upper plate on opposite page), but various derived forms are common including pure white to all black or brown birds. — Smaller and stockier than Wood Pigeon, beats wings faster in flight. Often glides with wings held in V-form. **Vo:** Crooning 'druoo-u' or 'oo-roo-coo'. **Hab:** Towns, villages and farms. In some areas small populations occupy coastal cliffs, these may include pure Rock Doves. **Bre:** The nest is a lose structure made of sticks and other vegetative matter. It is placed on buildings and also in caves on cliffs. Clutch is 2 eggs. The breeding season is prolonged but does not include the coldest winter months. **Dist:** Restricted to towns, villages and farms all over the country. Cliff breeders are known from Vestmannaeyjar east and north to Norðfjörður on the east coast. **Rem:** The Domestic Pigeon was introduced to Iceland in the 18th century by foreign merchants, mainly carrier pigeons in the beginning. **I:** Húsdúfa.

Feral pigeons, adult Rock Dove type in middle.

Feral (carrier) pigeons.

Collared Dove
Streptopelia decaocto 55

31–33 cm — Vagrant/Irregular breeder — Sexes identical — 3

An overall pale dove. Pale greyish-brown plumage. Narrow, black collar on hindneck. Pinkish breast. Pale-blue greater-coverts visible in flight. Dark primaries contrast with other parts. White corners on brownish uppertail and broad white terminal band on black undertail. *Juv* is duller, scaled above without neck-collar. Black bill, white cere. Red eyes and legs. — Stockier and paler than Turtle Dove, with longer tail and broader wings. Tail pattern also different. Flight fast, with clipped wing-beats. **Vo:** A deep crooning 'croo-dooh-coo'. Flight call a nasal, harsh 'kwurr'. **Hab:** Usually near inhabited areas, e.g. gardens, parks and forestry plantations, often seen on antennas. **Bre:** Nest made of sticks is placed in trees, often conifers. Clutch is 2 eggs. **Dist/Rem:** Has spread over much of Europe during this century. Rarer than the two other vagrant doves. First observed in Iceland in 1971. Since then has been observed irregularly and has made breeding attempts. Observed in all seasons, mainly from southwest to east. **I:** Tyrkjadúfa.

Adult:
1. Pale and stocky. Pale-blue greater coverts, dark primaries.
2. Black collar on hindneck
3. Rounded tail, mostly white underneath.

Turtle Dove
Streptopelia turtur 56

26–28 cm — Vagrant — Sexes identical — 3

Small, slim dove with longish tail. Grey head and outer wing-coverts, grey-brown back and rump. Orange-brown scapulars with black centres, giving the bird a scaly apperance above. Pink throat and breast, white belly. Rounded tail, dark, with broad white terminal band. *Ad* has a black- and white-striped patch on sides of neck. *Juv* more dull. Black bill and pale-yellow cere. Eyes yellow-brown, reddish orbital ring. Red legs. — Flies with jerky wing strokes. **Vo:** Call a repeated purring 'turr-turr-turr' or 'voor-r-r'. **Hab/Dist:** Vagrant from Europe, occuring from April to November, most frequent in summer and autumn. Reported from all parts of the country, most common in the east and southwest, encountered in parks, gardens and forestry plantations as well as on shores and in farmland. **I:** Turtildúfa.

Adult:
1. Slim body. Black and rufous above, with a scaly apperance.
2. Pinkish throat and breast.
3. Black and white striped patch on neck sides.
4. Dark, white-edged tail.

Collared Dove, adult.

Turtle Dove, adult.

Wood Pigeon

Columba palumbus

39–41 cm — Vagrant/Irregular breeder — Sexes identical — 4

The largest pigeon found in Iceland. *Ad* has white patches on sides of neck and white transverse bars on upperwing. Blue-grey plumage, glossy-green neck-sides, purple breast. Dark primaries and black terminal band on tail. Grey rump and uppertail, undertail white. *Juv* is duller and greyer than *ad* and lacks the neck pattern. Red, yellow-tipped bill. Pale-yellow eyes. Short, reddish legs. — Stocky, with realtively small head and long tail. Powerful flight with fast wing-beats. Noisy when taking off. **Vo:** A hoarse, cooing song, repeated 'coo-cooo-cu'. **Hab:** Woods, gardens, forestry plantations and farmland, also cliffs. **Bre:** Lays 2 eggs in stick nest placed in trees or on ledges in cliffs. **Dist:** Annual vagrant, mainly observed in spring and early summer (May-June) but also in other months (late April-November). Seen in all parts of Iceland, but most observations are from east to southwest. **Rem:** First recorded breeding in 1963, has bred few times since. **I:** Hringdúfa.

Adult:
1. *Large, grey-blue. Glossy-green neck-sides, purple breast.*
2. *White patch on neck-side.*
3. *White transverse bar on upperwing.*
4. *Black terminal band on tail.*

Wood Pigeon, adult.

Wood Pigeon, adult.

Waterfowl

and Other Wetland Birds

Two species of geese breed in Iceland: the Greylag Goose and the Pink-footed Goose. In addition to these, the White-fronted Goose, the Barnacle Goose and the Brent Goose pass through Iceland as migrants. The species that breed in Iceland divide the country amicably between them: the Greylag Goose, which has spread across the country over the past 50 years, keeps to the lowlands, while the Pink-footed Goose has occupied moorland and ledges in gullies in the highlands. One of the latter species' best-known settlements is on the wetlands to the south of the glacier Hofsjökull, where a breeding colony estimated at about 10,000 pairs is one of the largest colonies of geese in the world. These two Icelandic breeding stocks are thought to number over 100,000 pairs each. Reinforced by the three non-resident species, this makes for an abundant presence of geese. All of them seek food in grasslands, particularly uncultivated meadows, except for the Brent Goose, which feeds on Eelgrass and Common Saltmarsh-grass. Hayfields, and particularly newly cultivated land, are a conspicuous temptation for the hungry birds, which have a great energy requirement in order to keep their 3–4 kg bodies aloft and develop the 4–6 large eggs the females lay. Naturally their feeding causes some damage, though this is often greatly exaggerated. The White-fronted Goose, the Barnacle Goose and the Brent Goose follow established routes across the country. Brent Geese follow the west coast, while Barnacle Geese spread across the north of the country on their way north in the spring and across Skaftafellssýsla in the autumn, and White-fronted Geese move across the south and west of the country. Geese, ducks and swans loose all their flight feathers once each year, so becoming completely incapable of flight. In the past, Icelandic geese were herded together into special pens and killed, while swans were chased and clubbed to death. Geese are protected between 15th March and 20th August, and the Brent Goose is protected all year round.

Ducks are divided into two categories, dabbling ducks and diving ducks, in addition to the Mergansers. The sexes are well differentiated in all species, the drakes being both larger and more impressive in appearance. At the end of the breeding period, ducks moult and lose the ability to fly, the drakes taking on an appearance similar to that of the females. As autumn approaches they take on their coloured plumage, which they retain until the next breeding season. *Dabbling ducks* live on grass, grazing on land and in lakes. They have specula on the secondaries, clearly defined rectangles with beautiful blue or green colouring, frequently with a metallic tinge. They tend to inhabit shallow ponds or keep to the edges of deeper lakes, slow-moving rivers or moorlands. They up-end in shallow water and tear up vegetation with the sharp "nail" at the end of their bills. Along the edge of their bills there are sieves which come into play during feeding. Meanwhile the ducks paddle or dabble with their feet (hence the name of the group, dabbling ducks). Dabbling ducks are able to dive when frightened, and the young are capable divers. These ducks take off very quickly from water, without an initial run. *Diving ducks* keep mostly to deep lakes, and are therefore not encountered as frequently as dabblers. Some stay on the sea. They have more powerful legs than the dabbling ducks, and they are situated further back on their bodies. There is a lobe on the hind toe which is not connected to the others by webbing. These ducks live mostly on

invertebrates, for which they dive. Their wings are shorter than those of the dabbling ducks, and so their take-off is correspondingly clumsier, necessitating a considerable run on the surface of the water. Their wings are either of a uniform colour, without a speculum, or the speculum is of a single colour, generally white. More of the rear part of the bird is under water when they swim than is the case with the dabbling ducks. Their bills are similar, also being provided with a sharp nail. Both dabbling ducks and diving ducks have a saddle-shaped bill, flat or slightly raised.

The *Mergansers* comprise the Red-breasted Merganser and the Goosander. They beat their wings quickly in flight and never glide, with their necks and heads extended stiffly from their slender bodies. The edge of the tail is curved. The bill is red, with a sharp hooked nail. Rows of backward-pointing barbs run along the edges of the bill, which make it possible for the birds to catch and hold slippery fish. The feet are red. These birds are capable of diving to considerable depths.

Of the third group of water-birds, the *Swans*, only one species is found in Iceland: the Whooper Swan.

Included here with the waterfowl are the wetland birds *Grebes* and *Divers*. *Grebes* live on lakes and on the sea. They are clumsy in flight but are agile divers. They have practically no tail, the legs projecting far behind in flight. Grebes have lobed toes. Their beaks are short and dagger-shaped. Grebes often build floating nests. The *Divers* (the Red-throated Diver and the Great Northern Diver) are powerful and bulky swimmers with great diving ability. They frequently swim half-submerged with only their heads projecting from the water. In flight, the shoulders are the highest part of the body, and the legs project beyond the short tail. They fly at considerable heights. Divers have long knife-like beaks. Their legs are situated right at the back of the body, and they are unable to walk. They build their nests on the banks of lakes and ponds, crawling to and from the water on their bellies.

Greylag Goose
Anser anser 58

Adult:
1. All orange bill.
2. Brown-grey head, neck and upper-back.
3. Greyish-pink legs.

75–90 cm — Breeder — Sexes similar, ♂ slightly larger — 7

The largest Icelandic goose. All brown-grey, darker above and on neck. Paler below, except dark flanks. Sometimes with dark spots on breast and belly. Like other grey geese with white vent, undertail and uppertail coverts. Pale-grey forewings and rump conspicuous in flight. Difficult to distinguish between *ad* and *juv.* Orange bill. Dark eyes with orange orbital rings. Greyish-pink legs. — Gregarious most of the year except breeding pairs. Flight direct and powerful. Flies in V-shaped flocks or lines. A good swimmer. Larger and paler than other grey geese in Iceland. **Vo:** Variable, mostly loud and deep nasal gabbling. **Hab:** Breeds mainly below the 300 m contour line, esp. in marshes, on vegetated islets and on banks of rivers and lakes; also in heathlands, on islands in fjords, etc., often in scattered colonies. Outside breeding season prefers cultivated areas like potato fields and hayfields, as well as wetlands when migrating. Moults on rivers, fjords and lakes. **Bre:** Nest is a depression in ground, usually well hidden in tall growth, lined with vegetation, feathers and down. Clutch is 4–8 eggs, laid mainly in early May. **Dist:** Common breeder in lowland areas all over the country. Winters in Britain and Ireland. A few hundred birds are sedentary and winter in Reykjavík, very few elsewhere. **Rem:** The population has been increasing for the last decades, from c. 25,000 birds in 1952 to c. 125,000 birds in 1989. **I:** Grágæs.

In flight:
1. Larger and paler than other grey geese, with direct and powerful flight.
2. Pale forewing.

Greylag Goose, adult.

Greylag Geese in flight.

Pink-footed Goose

Anser brachyrhynchus   **59**

60–75 cm — Breeder — Sexes similar, but ♂ slightly larger — 7

One of the characteristic birds of the Central Highlands. Head
and neck coffee-brown, contrasting with blue-grey upperparts.
Paler and slightly pinkish on breast and lower neck. White
undertail. Dark-streaked flanks down to belly. Blue-grey
forewings, not as pale as on Greylag. *Ad* and *juv* similar, but *juv*
darker. Short bill, with variable pink and black colouration,
black nail. Brown eyes. Pink legs. — Gregarious during all
seasons. Flies with fast and fluid wing-beats in more compact

*1. Short bill, pinkish on front and black
on top. Black nail.*
2. Dark-brown head and neck.
3. Pink legs.
4. Blue-grey (pale) forewings.

flocks than other grey geese. Note also small head and short neck in flight. **Vo:** Similar to
Greylag, but higher pitched, not as cackling as White-fronted Goose. Most common is a
musical short 'ung-unk' or 'ang-ank'. **Hab:** Wet highland oases, river gorges, canyons and
banks of rivers are the main breeding habitats. In spring and autumn it stages both in the
highlands and in lowland areas (esp. in spring), mainly on cultivated fields. **Bre:** Nests on
ground or on cliff ledges. The same nest scrapes used year after year, gradually increasing
in size. Clutch is 4–7 eggs, laid in late May. **Dist:** Mainly in highland areas, but is extending
its range down along some of the major rivers. Winters in Scotland and N-England. Many
non-breeders moult in Greenland and Greenland population migrates through Iceland.
Rem: The Iceland-Greenland population has been increasing for the last decades, from
23,000 birds in 1952 to 200,000 in 1989. **I:** Heiðagæs.

White-fronted Goose

Anser albifrons   **60**

65–78 cm — Passage migrant — Sexes similar, ♂ slightly
larger — 7

The darkest of the Icelandic grey geese, a passage bird seen in
spring and autumn. Grey-brown, with pale bars above and dark
bars on flanks. Dark forewing characteristic in flight. *Ad* more or
less barred and spotted black on belly, sometimes almost wholly
black. White patch above base of bill. *Juv* lacks the black stripes
on belly and the white patch on forehead. Orange-yellow bill.
Brown eyes. Orange legs. — Gregarious during all seasons.
Behaves like other grey geese but takes off faster, is slimmer
and more agile in flight, and flock formation looser. Note also
darker and narrower wings. Swims well. **Vo:** Higher pitched,
more musical and gabbling than other grey geese. Mainly heard
in flight. **Hab:** In Iceland prefers cultivated fields, meadows,

Adult:
1. Orange bill. White forehead.
2. Black bars on belly.
3. Orange legs.
4. Dark (fore)wings.

Note:
*Juvenile in autumn has uniform brown
plumage, and lacks white forehead
patch and black on belly. Most have the
patch in first spring.*

bogs and marshland. Breeds on tundra marshes. **Dist/Rem:** The
subspecies *A.a. flavirostris*, which breeds in West-Greenland
and winters mainly in Ireland and Scotland, migrates through
Iceland and stages in lowland areas, from Snæfellsnes in the
west, south and east to Vatnajökull. The population has fluctuated
in size and was c. 28,000 birds in 1989. **I:** Blesgæs.

Pink-footed Geese, pair with young, the gander (♂) on the left.

White-fronted Geese in flight, adults.

Barnacle Goose

Branta leucopsis   61

58–69 cm — Passage migrant/Rare breeder — Sexes similar, ♂ slightly larger — 6

1. *Short, black bill.*
2. *Forehead, ear-coverts and chin white.*
   Black eye-stripe (lacking on photo).
3. *Black neck and breast.*
4. *Black legs.*

One of the two *Branta* species migrating through Iceland. Best distinguished by clear contrast between black and white in plumage, white face, chin and forehead. Black crown, nape, neck and breast. Upperparts dark- to blue-grey with white-edged black bars. Wings look grey in flight. Pale-grey underparts. White tail coverts, black-edged tail. Small, black bill; black eye-stripe (lacking on photo). Brown eyes. Black legs. — Larger than Brent Goose, beats wings slower. Looser flock formations in flight compared with other geese. **Vo:** Rapid barking 'ark' or 'gnuk'. **Hab:** In Iceland prefers marshes and hayfields near sea in spring, also highland, heathland and oases in autumn. Breeds colonially in the Arctic on steep cliffs and rocky river ravines. **Bre:** Nest scrape is lined with down and dry grass, 4–5 eggs. **Dist:** The NE-Greenland population, currently 35,000 birds (1988), migrates through Iceland and winters in the British Isles. The main staging areas in spring are in the central north and in the southern parts of the Central Highlands and Skaftafellssýslur in autumn. **Rem:** A few pairs have bred for 20 years, mainly on small islands in Breiðafjörður but also in other areas. Sometimes pairs with Greylags or Pink-feets. **I:** Helsingi.

Brent Goose

Branta bernicla   62

56–61 cm — Passage migrant — Sexes similar — 6

Adult:
1. *Short, bluish-black bill.*
2. *White transverse bars at sides of neck.*
3. *Black head, neck and breast.*
4. *White tail, black tailband.*

Note:
Juvenile lacks the neck stripes.

The smallest Icelandic goose. Sooty-black head, neck and breast. White patches on sides of neck. Dark brown-grey back and wings. Pale grey-brown belly, upperbreast and flanks, whiter towards rear. Slightly barred flanks. *Juv* lacks neck patches. Short blackish bill and legs. Dark-brown eyes. — Flies fast, with quick wing-beats. Forms irregular flocks, seldom in V-formation. Note also short neck and small size, resembling Mallard. Swims well with raised tail and up-ends when feeding in water. **Vo:** Usually silent except in flight, then uttering a guttural, soft 'rronk'. **Hab:** More coastal than other geese; frequents mudflats and sheltered bays rich in Eelgrass (*Zostera marina*). Breeds in loose colonies in Arctic on tundra or islets off coast. **Dist:** Greenlandic Brent and part of the Canadian Brent population (*B.b. hrota*), wintering in Ireland, are passage migrants in Iceland. The main staging areas are in western Iceland, mainly Faxaflói and southern part of Breiðafjörður. **Rem:** The population numbered c. 20,000 birds in 1989. The Brent is totally protected in Iceland. **I:** Margæs.

126

Barnacle Goose

Brent Goose, adult.

Mallard

Anas platyrhynchos

63

50–65 cm — Breeder — Sexes dissimilar — 5

Male:
1. *Green head. Yellow-green bill.*
2. *White neck-collar.*
3. *Chestnut breast.*
4. *Blue speculum, bordered by black and white lines.*

Common dabbling duck. ♂ is unmistakable, with glossy dark-green head and neck, separated from chestnut breast by white collar. Pale-grey, dully vermiculated body and wings, darker above than below. Black undertail and vent. Whitish tail with 2 black curled central feathers. Olive-yellow bill, black nail. In *eclipse* darker than ♀, esp. on head, and bill yellower. ♀ is uniformly mottled brown on body, paler head and belly. Head and neck finely streaked, with darker crown and supercilium. Dark, greenish bill with orange spots on upper mandible, dark nail. *Both sexes* have a metallic dark-blue speculum, bordered with black and white lines, diagnostic in flight. Dark eyes. Orange legs. — The largest and the most robust of the dabbling ducks, easily distinguished on water, land and in the air. Flies fast with shallow wing-beats. Rises quickly from water with steep ascent. Good walker, with horizontal posture on land. **Vo:** Usually noisy. Rough quack is common. ♀ usually louder, ♂ utters more whistling notes. **Hab:** Breeds in a wide range of habitats, though mostly in lowland wetlands, often near human habitation. Moults mainly on lakes or ponds bordered by sedge. Winters on coast; also inland where waters remain open in winter. **Bre:** Nest is

Duck.

Female:
1. *Greenish and orange bill.*
2. *Mottled-brown body.*
3. *Orange legs.*
4. *Blue speculum as on drakes.*

usually well hidden in vegetation, between stones or tussocks etc. Nest is made of grass, lined with down. Clutch is 6–12 eggs, laid late April into June. **Dist:** Found in suitable habitats all over the country, except for the Central Highlands, where it is rare. **I:** Stokkönd.

Mallard, male (drake).

Mallard, female (duck).

Teal

Anas crecca

64

34–38 cm — Breeder — Sexes dissimilar — 4

The smallest Icelandic duck. ♂ has a chestnut head and neck, green patch from eye to nape, edged by narrow buffish line. Yellowish breast with dark spots. Body otherwise grey except for black rump and vent, latter with creamy patches on both sides. Black and white scapulars, showing sidelines when wings are folded. At a distance looks all dark with darker head, but undertail patches often visible. ♀ is mottled grey- and yellow-brown, looks like a miniature Mallard. Note head pattern. *Both sexes* have white belly. Metallic green and black speculum, broad white edge in front, narrow behind. Dark-grey bill, some yellow at sides of upper mandible on female. Brown eyes. Grey legs, darker webs. — Commonly found in small flocks or pairs. Small and compact, with rounded head and short neck. Narrow wings, flies fast and low, often in tight groups, suggesting waders. Rises fast with steep ascent, shy. **Vo:** ♂ utters a short whistling and musical, bell-like 'kriit' or 'preep'. ♀'s call is similar to Mallard, a harsh quack. **Hab:** In summer the Teal prefers lowland wetlands, e.g. vegetated ponds and wet sedge-fens and mires. In winter found on rivers, ponds and openings on lakes, kept open by thermal springs, also on sheltered coastal coves.

Male:
1. *Green side-patches on chestnut head, bordered with thin yellow line.*
2. *Green speculum, bordered with white.*
3. *Grey body. Paler breast.*

Note yellowish vent-patches.

Drake.

Female:
1. *Very small duck, mottled-brown and buff.*
2. *Green speculum, white borders.*
3. *Greyish bill and legs.*

Bre: Nest similar to other dabbling ducks, usually well hidden in vegetation. Clutch is 8–11 eggs, laid in May. **Dist:** Breeds in suitable habitats in lowland areas all over Iceland. Also found in highland oases, but rare. Winters mainly in the British Isles and in W-Europe. A few hundred winter in the southwest. **I:** Urtönd.

Teal, male (drake).

Teal, female (duck).

Wigeon
Anas penelope

65

45–51 cm — Breeder — Sexes dissimilar — 4

Medium sized dabbling duck with short neck, small bill, slightly rounded head, pointed tail and long narrow wings. ♂ chestnut on head and neck with creamy-yellow forehead and crown. Glossy patch behind eye. Vermiculated grey body, pinkish-red breast, white belly and vent. Wedge-shaped black tail and tail coverts, with paler edges and rump. Black and grey scapulars. White forewings (secondary coverts) distinctive in flight and show as white band along side when wing is folded. In *eclipse plumage* darker than female and wing band still obvious. *First year ♂* lack white wing panels. ♀ grey or rufous, mottled-brown, flanks cinnamon and forewings greyish-brown. White belly. *Both sexes* have dark-green speculum with metallic sheen, duller on ♀, edged with black (♂) and white (♀). Grey-blue, short bill with black tip. Brown eyes. Blue-grey to brownish legs, darker webs. — Gregarious during all seasons. Shape and white forewing of male distinctive. Flies fast with rapid wing-beats. Swims rather low on water, with retracted neck, seldom up-ends. Often feeds on land. **Vo:** ♂ has a high whistle 'wheee-oo', ♀'s call is low purring growl 'karr-karr'.

Adult male:
1. Cream-coloured forehead and crown on chestnut head.
2. White secondary coverts.
3. Black and green speculum.
4. Grey body, white belly and pinkish-red breast.

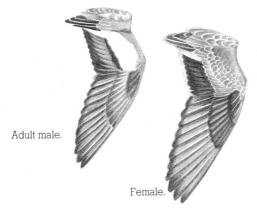

Adult male.

Female.

Female:
1. Grey-brown body. Often more rufous than other dabbling ducks.
2. Tail rather long and pointed.
3. Short, blue-grey bill of both sexes. Black tip.

Hab: In summer shallow, eutrophic lakes and ponds. Resides mainly on sheltered coastal coves in winter. **Bre:** Nests in marshes and moorland, nest well hidden among tussocks, in heather and scrubs. Clutch is 6–10 eggs, laid in early June. **Dist:** Main breeding areas are in N- and NE-Iceland, e.g. the Lake Mývatn area, rarer in other regions. About 70% of population winters in Britain, the rest in W-Europe and to some extent on the eastern seaboard of N-America. A few hundred birds winter in SW-Iceland. **Rem:** Grazes more on land than other ducks. **I:** Rauðhöfðaönd.

Wigeon, male (drake).

Wigeon, female (duck).

Gadwall

Anas strepera 66

46–56 cm — Breeder — Sexes dissimilar — 5

A rare duck, mostly found in northeast Iceland. ♂ grey, browner on head and neck, with heavily vermiculated blackish breast. Brownish scapulars. Black stern with paler tail. White belly. Dark-grey bill, except when in *eclipse plumage*, then drake is very similar to duck. ♀ reminiscent of ♀ Mallard but is smaller and more slenderly built, has rounder head, and is greyer with different colour of bill and speculum. Dark culmen and orange sides on narrow bill. *Both sexes* have white speculum bordered with black and rusty patch on wing coverts, duller on ♀. Dark-brown eyes. Orange legs, grey webs. — Found in pairs or small groups, usually among other dabbling ducks. Flies fast; wing formation similar to Wigeon. **Vo:** ♀'s call is a loud quack, ♂'s a low whistle. **Hab:** Sedge-mires and fertile bogs, shallow lakes and pools in lowlands. **Bre:** Nests near water in thick vegetation, under tussocks, bushes or tall grass. Nest scrape is lined with grass and down. Clutch is 7–12 eggs, laid late May into June. **Dist:** Rare outside the Mývatn-Laxá area, where c. 200 pairs breed. Scattered pairs found in good waterfowl areas in all parts of Iceland, e.g. in the vicinity of Reykjavík. Chiefly migratory, winters in Ireland and Britain. Sometimes a few birds winter in Reykjavík and at Lake Mývatn. **I:** Gargönd.

Male:
1. *Grey-brown head and neck.*
2. *Brownish scapular. Grey breast, back and flanks*
3. *White belly.*
4. *Black stern.*

Drake.

Female:
1. *Narrow, grey bill, edged with orange.*
2. *Both sexes have white speculum, edged with black and rusty bands on wing coverts.*
3. *Reminiscent of female Mallard, smaller and more slenderly built with rounder head.*

Gadwall, male (drake).

Gadwall, females (ducks).

Pintail

Anas acuta

67

51–76 cm — Breeder — Sexes dissimilar, ♂ c. 70 cm including tail, ♀ c. 54 cm — 5

Male:
1. *Coffee-brown head and neck. White stripe on sides of slender neck.*
2. *Long, narrow, black central tail feathers.*
3. *White breast and belly. Grey flanks and back.*
4. *Both sexes have green (♂) or brown (♀) speculum, bordered with white and brown.*

Rare but widespread wetland duck, slender built with long neck. At distance ♂ looks grey with white breast and dark head. Coffee-brown head and chin, darker nape and hindneck. White breast, belly and foreneck; white stripes on neck sides extend up to head. Vermiculated grey sides, back and primary coverts. Black rump and undertail coverts, bordered with white, greyish-white tail with two long black central tail feathers. Black scapulars, bordered with white. In *eclipse plumage* similar to ♀, but greyer above. Grey-blue bill, black base, culmen and nail. ♀ similar to other dabbling ducks, but paler and greyer, slimmer, with longer neck and pointed tail. Crescent marks on flanks. White belly. Grey bill. *Both sexes* have metallic-green speculum, with white proximal borders and brown distal borders, duller and browner on ♀. Yellow-brown eyes. Grey legs with darker webs. — Usually found in pairs or small flocks. Shape distinctive. Shy; strong flight with rapid beats, narrow pointed wings. Floats high on water. A good walker. Acts more like Wigeon than Mallard. **Vo:** Rather silent, ♂ utters a low nasal whistle, ♀ a low quack and growl. **Hab:** Wet sedge-mires, fens and eutrophic lakes and ponds bordered with marshes. Found both in lowland and in highland regions. The few overwintering birds are found on coasts. **Bre:** Nest is commonly more open than nests of other dabbling ducks, lined with grass, down and feathers. Clutch is 7–9 eggs, laid mid-May to early June. **Dist:** Found breeding all over the country, but most common in the north and northeast. Winters mainly in Britain and Ireland, few recovered further south-east in Europe, also in Greenland and Canada. **I:** Grafönd.

Female:
1. *Both sexes have grey bill and legs.*
2. *Pointed tail.*
3. *Paler, more slender shape and thinner neck than female Mallard.*

Drake.

Pintail, male (drake).

Pintail, pair, female (duck) on the left.

Shoveller

Anas clypeata

68

Male:
1. *Long, spatulate, grey-black bill.*
2. *Dark-green head. White neck and breast.*
3. *Pale-blue forewing patches. Green speculum.*
4. *Chestnut flanks and belly.*

44–52 cm — Breeder — Sexes dissimilar — 5

This unmistakable duck with its huge bill is the rarest of the regular breeding ducks in Iceland. Glossy-green head and neck of ♂, white on breast extends back to scapulars and front of vent. Chestnut flanks and belly. Black centre of back, rump and undertail coverts. Long black scapulars with white centre. In *eclipse plumage* resembles ♀ but darker above with paler blue forewing. Black-grey bill. Yellow eyes. ♀ similar to other dabbling ducks, except for huge bill, more buffish-pink paler areas and upperwing pattern. Grey-brown bill edged with orange. Brown to yellow eyes. *Both sexes* have a distinctive pale-blue forewing and green speculum bordered with white bar; duller colours in female. Orange legs. — Compact, medium sized, short-necked duck, forehead flattened out to heavy spatula-shaped bill. Rather shy, found single, in pairs or small groups. Small wings sit backward on body. Heavy in flight and sits low on water. Paddles with outstretched head in mud or shallow water, also up-ends. **Vo:** Usually quiet. ♂ has a low, double, staccato 'vack-ack'; ♀ quacks. **Hab:** Eutrophic wetlands, usually not far from coast. **Bre:** Nests in tall vegetation, usually near water. Nest is made of grass and sedge, lined with down. Clutch of 8–12 eggs laid probably in late May. **Dist/Rem:** The Shoveller is a new immigrant to Iceland. It was known as a rare vagrant, but in 1934 breeding was proved. It is known to breed in some wetland areas, mainly in the north and northeast (e.g. Lake Mývatn), but also in the south and west. The breeding population has been estimated to be less than 100 pairs. Wintering quarters are not known, but assumed to be in the British Isles. **I:** Skeiðönd.

Female:
1. *Long, grey-brown spatulate bill, edged with orange.*
2. *Buffish-brown barred plumage.*
3. *Grey-blue forewing. Green speculum.*
4. *Both sexes have orange legs.*

Drake.

Shoveller, male (drake).

Shoveller, female (duck).

Scaup

Aythya marila

69

42–51 cm — Breeder — Sexes dissimilar — 4

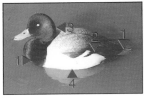

Male:
1. *Black in front and rear.*
2. *Grey above, white wing-bars.*
3. *Dark-green head. Blue-grey bill.*
4. *White flanks and belly.*

Common diving duck. At a distance ♂ looks black in front and rear, pale in middle. Glossy dark-green head, black breast, white flanks and belly. Vermiculated grey back and scapulars, black rump and undertail coverts, grey-brown tail. Grey-brown upperwing, with white wing-bar on most of flight feathers. Duller in *eclipse plumage*, black turning brown and often some white marks on head and breast. ♀ is dark-brown on head, neck and breast. Reddish-brown back and scapulars, often vermiculated grey. Grey-brown stern. Yellow-brown tinged flanks, white belly. White wing-bar, like male, on dark-brown upperwings. White patch around base of bill, in breeding plumage also a pale patch on ear coverts. *Juv* like ♀, but uniformly darker with darker eyes. *Both sexes* have pale underwings. Grey-blue bill, black nail. Yellow eyes. Grey-blue legs, darker webs. — Gregarious during all seasons. Flies fast with quick wing-beats. Swims low in water and dives well, runs on water when taking off. Seldom seen on land. Best distinguished from Tufted Duck by different shape of head (no crest, higher forehead), ♂ by grey back and ♀ by size, paler colour, and larger face patch and ear patch in summer. **Vo:** Rather silent; ♀ has a growling,

Drake.

Female:
1. *White patch around base of bill.*
2. *Mostly brown body. Paler flanks, tinged white or grey. White belly and wing-bars.*
3. *Both sexes have short blue-grey legs.*

harsh 'kerr', male a soft whistle in courtship period. Sometimes vocal in flight. **Hab:** Breeds near lakes and pools, both in highland and lowland areas. In winter in sheltered coves. **Bre:** Nests close to water, often colonial and associated with Black-headed Gull or Arctic Tern colonies. The nest is a depression lined with grass and down and well hidden in sedges, scrubs or other vegetation. Clutch is 8–11 eggs, laid late May to late June. **Dist:** Breeds in all parts of the country, rare in Vestfirðir and the Central Highlands. Most abundant in the Lake Mývatn area. Winters in W-Europe, mainly the British Isles and Netherlands. Few flocks winter annually in SW-Iceland. **Rem:** See Tufted Duck. **I:** Duggönd.

Scaup, male (drake).

Scaup, female (duck).

Tufted Duck

Aythya fuligula

70

40–47 cm — Breeder — Sexes dissimilar — 4

Male:
1. *Both sexes have blue-grey bill with black nail.*
2. *Drooping crest from nape.*
3. *All black, except for white flanks, belly and wing-bars.*

The most common diving duck of lowland areas. ♂ looks black at distance, except for white flanks. Round, glossy dark-blue head, black drooping crest from nape. White flanks, belly, underwings and wing-bars; other feathered parts black or brownish-black. In *eclipse plumage* like ♀, but darker except for sides and underparts and has no white face marks. Barred-brown flanks in *1st winter.* ♀ is variable, dark-brown above, mottled paler flanks, white belly. Most have white spot at base of bill, crest much shorter than ♂♂. White wing-bars, grey-brown to white undertail. Undertail and face patch brighter in winter plumage. *Juv* darker, at first with brown and then paler eyes. *Both sexes* have blue-grey or dark-grey bill with black nail. Bright yellow eyes. Grey-blue legs, dark webs. — Gregarious. Acts much as Scaup. Best distinguished from Scaup by slimmer body, different head-shape (more rounded with crest) and darker plumage, ♀ also by face marks. **Vo:** Similar to Scaup (q.v.). Usually silent. **Hab:** Eutrophic, richly vegetated, shallow lowland lakes and ponds in summer. Wintering birds favour mostly freshwater, ice-free lakes and rivers, sometimes coastal. **Bre:** Nest selection similar to Scaup. Clutch is 7–12 eggs, laid late

Drake.

Female:
1. *Most have tiny white patch at base of bill.*
2. *Dark-brown body, paler flanks.*
3. *Broad white wing-bar.*
4. *Trace of crest on nape.*

May to late June. **Dist:** Occurs in lowland areas all over Iceland, but rare in the northwest (Vestfirðir) and mostly absent in the Central Higlands. Overwintering birds found in the southwest, south and on Lake Mývatn. Main winter quarters in W-Europe, chiefly Ireland and also Britain. **Rem:** First recorded at the end of last century and is now probably the most common duck species breeding in Iceland, excluding the Eider. Has replaced the Scaup as the most common duck on Lake Mývatn. **I:** Skúfönd.

Tufted Duck, male (drake).

Tufted Duck, female (duck).

Pochard

Aythya ferina

71

Male:
1. *Chestnut head and neck.*
2. *Black breast and stern.*
3. *Pale-grey above and on flanks, white belly.*

42–49 cm — Annual vagrant/Irregular breeder — Sexes dissimilar — 4

Medium-sized diving duck. From distance *both sexes* look dark-fronted with pale body. ♂ has a conspicuous chestnut head and neck, black breast and stern. In between the body is mostly pale-grey. White belly. Duller and browner in *eclipse plumage*. Reddish eyes. ♀ is buff-brown on head, neck and mantle but slightly darker on breast and crown. Buffish areas on cheeks, chin, throat and around base of bill, often with similar coloured eye stripe. Brown, grey-tinged back, scapular and flanks. White belly. Dark-brown stern. Brown eyes, reddish in summer. *Both sexes* have grey upperwings with paler-grey, ill defined, broad wing-bar on flight feathers. Dark-grey bill, black at end, blue-grey band across middle, duller on ♀. — Found single, in pairs or small parties. Long bill, flat forehead and high crown distinctive. Stocky and rather heavy on water. **Vo:** Similar to Scaup and Tufted Duck. Generally quiet. ♂ utters soft whistles during courtship, ♀ a harsh growl, mainly in flight. **Hab:** In summer eutrophic lakes, in winter mainly coastal. **Dist/Rem:** First recorded breeding at Lake Mývatn in 1954, seen there in most years and occasionally with young. Not infrequently observed in SW- and S-Iceland. **I:** Skutulönd.

Drake.

Female:
1. *Brown head, neck and breast.*
2. *Buff-brown areas on throat, cheeks and at base of bill.*
3. *Brown, grey-tinged back and flanks.*

Note:
Both sexes have a blue-grey band on dark-grey bill and grey wing-bars.

Pochard, male (drake).

Pochard, female (duck).

Harlequin Duck

Histrionicus histrionicus

72

38–45 cm — Breeder — Sexes dissimilar — 4

Small, dark diving duck, the characteristic bird of white-water rivers and coasts. ♂ is picturesque, richly coloured, body is dark-blue and rufous pattern, with black-edged white stripes on head and body. Main colour is grey-blue. Rufous lines on crown; chestnut flanks down to reddish-grey belly. Dark wings, tiny and short white wing-bars. White lines on scapulars. At distance looks dark with white marks. In *eclipse plumage* like ♀, but darker with trace of white breast band and white in wings. *Young ♂♂* duller than adults. ♀ is uniformly blackish-brown, mottled-brown on breast and flanks, whitish belly. White spots on ear coverts, in front of eyes and around base of bill. No wing marks. *Both sexes* have a short, lead-blue bill. Brown eyes. Legs grey-blue to greenish (♀), darker webs. Bill and legs duller in ♀. — Small, short-necked diving duck with short, narrow bill, high forehead and pointed tail. Tame and gregarious; outside breeding season mostly in small, compact flocks. Flies fast with rapid wing-beats and tumbles, low over water. Rarely takes short cuts overland, but follows every curve of river, even flying under bridges. Swims buoyantly with bobbing head and tail often cocked, like bouncing on current or surf. Dives easily in turbulent water, sometimes from rocks or flight. **Vo:** A squeaky call. ♂ utters a low whistle ending in a trill, ♀ a harsh croak, but usually silent. **Hab:** In summer spring-fed, turbulent rivers and lake outlets, rich with blackflies. ♂♂ moult at sea. Winters on coasts, staying in rocky surfy areas. **Bre:** On river banks or on islands in rivers. Nest is hidden among rocks, scrubs or other vegetation, made of grass and twigs, lined with down. Clutch is 5–7 eggs, laid late May to mid-June. **Dist:** Found in suitable

Male:
1. Both sexes have short, lead-blue bill.
2. Grey-blue, with white streaks on head and body.
3. Rufous flanks.

Female:
1. White spots on lores, forehead and ear coverts.
2. Dark-brown body and wings, without wingmarks. White belly.

Drake.

habitats all over Iceland. Sedentary. **Rem:** Iceland is the only European breeding haunt for this delightful species. Strictly protected in all seasons. **I:** Straumönd.

146

Harlequin Duck, male (drake).

Harlequins Ducks, pair, female (duck) on the right.

Long-tailed Duck

Clangula hyemalis   73

40–60 cm — Breeder — Sexes dissimilar, ♂ c. 60 cm with long tail feathers, ♀ c. 40 cm — 4 (— 5)

The characteristic diving duck of highland lakes and pools. The only duck with white body in winter and uniform dark wings, darker in summer. Complex plumage sequence. In *summer* ♂ is dark-brown on head, neck, breast and above, with whitish face patches and buff-edged scapulars. White flanks, belly, vent and tail except for long black central tail-feathers. In *eclipse plumage* similar, but duller and lacks long tail-feathers. In *winter* much paler, white on head and neck, with grey smudge around eyes and dark-brown cheek-patch. Sooty-brown breast-band, joining on mantle and back to tail feathers, forming a Y on upperparts in flight. Whitish, conspicuous scapulars. Black base of bill and nail, pinkish-red in between. Yellow to red eyes. ♀ *summer* sooty-brown on head and upper breast, with grey in front of eyes and whitish eye-stripe and neck. Otherwise similar to ♂, except for shorter and greyer scapulars and no tail-streamers. *Winter plumage* is slightly paler, brown colours greyer and more white on head and throat. Slate-grey bill. Brown eyes. *Both sexes* have plain, dark-brown wings and blue-grey legs with darker webs. Plumage of *imm*, and *ad* in spring and autumn variable. — Gregarious. Rapid flight with peculiar wing-beats. Flies in irregular flocks or lines, tumbling from side to side showing alternately dark and white, usually low over water. A good diver and buoyant swimmer; ♂ often raises tail when swimming. Rather tame but restless and commonly diving or taking off. **Vo:** Usually vocal, esp. ♂, uttering a loud, nasal yodel 'a-a-aahuu','ow-ow-owdelee' etc. ♀'s is a low yelping quack. **Hab:** In summer inland on lakes and pools, also on brackish coastal pools or lowland lakes. On coastal waters in winter. **Bre:** Nest, usually close to water, a small depression in ground in thick vegetation, lined with grass and down. Clutch is 6–9 eggs, laid late May to June. **Dist:** Breeds in highland areas all over Iceland, but also in lowland areas, mainly in the north; rarer in the south. Overwinters at sea, both on coast but also in deeper water feeding on krill. Some migrate to SW-Greenland in winter, but large numbers from other Arctic areas, winter in Icelandic waters. **I:** Hávella.

Drake in winter.

Adult male, summer:
1. *Dark-brown head, neck and breast, except for pale eye-patch.*
2. *Brown above, white below.*
3. *Long, black, central tail-feathers.*

Adult female, summer:
4. *Pale eye-stripe, dark head and white neck.*

Adult male, winter:
2. *White head and neck, dark patch on cheeks. Black and pink bill in all seasons.*
3. *Whitish scapulars.*

Adult female, winter:
1. *Grey bill in all seasons.*
4. *Paler on head and throat, with greyer body than in summer.*

Note:
Both sexes have uniformly dark wings all year round.

Long-tailed Ducks, pair in summer, drake below.

Long-tailed Ducks in winter, drake on the left, two ducks on the right.

Barrow's Goldeneye

Bucephala islandica

74

42–53 cm — Breeder — Sexes dissimilar, ♂ larger — 5

The characteristic duck of the Lake Mývatn area. At a distance ♂ seems dark above and pale below. Glossy purple-black head and throat, white crescent spot between eye and bill. White neck, breast and belly. Black back and stern. Line of white spots on black scapulars, black wings with white speculum and median secondary coverts. In *eclipse plumage* like ♀, but darker head and black bill. *Imm* ♂ browner above and below, with ill-defined loral crescent. Slate-black bill. ♀ has chocolate-brown head, conspicuous white neck collar. Mottled, dark-grey body, paler on breast and flanks than above. Whitish belly. Black bill, more or less yellow near tip. Wing-pattern similar to males. *Both sexes* have yellow eyes, orange legs and dark webs. — Large, oval head, short bill, steep forehead, flat crown and bulging sides are distinctive. Larger and bulkier than Goldeneye. Wings produce whistling sound in flight. Tame, lively and restless, esp. in display. **Vo:** Usually silent. Harsh, grunting notes during courtship. **Hab:** Freshwater lakes and spring-fed rivers. **Bre:** Nests in holes or crevices in rocks or lava, sometimes in thick vegetation, buildings or nest-boxes. Nest a depression lined with down. Clutch is 8–11 eggs, laid mid-May to June. **Dist:** The only European breeding grounds of this species are in NE-Iceland, mainly at Lake Mývatn and Laxá River. Winters on the breeding grounds and on ice-free lakes and rivers in the south. **I:** Húsönd.

Adult male:
1. *Black head, white crescent spot in front of eyes.*
2. *White spots on scapulars.*
Adult female:
3. *Coffee-brown head, white neck-collar, grey body, white belly.*
Both sexes:
4. *White wing-square (speculum) broken by transverse line near front.*

Drake.

Goldeneye

Bucephala clangula

75

42–50 cm — Winter visitor/summer visitor — Sexes dissimilar, ♂ slightly larger — 5

At a distance ♂ looks nearly all white except for dark head. White circular spot at base of bill. White scapulars. ♀ similar to Barrow's, but smaller, head more triangular-shaped, forehead not as steep and neck collar broader. *Both sexes* have large white wing-patches, larger than Barrow's. Bill, eyes and legs similar to Barrow's, except for narrower yellow ring on bill in ♀. **Vo:** Similar to Barrow's. **Hab/Dist:** In winter ice-free lakes and rivers, often in company of Barrow's, but also coastal coves in the southwest. In summer few birds found with Barrow's, mainly at Lake Mývatn. **I:** Hvinönd.

Adult male:
1. *Round, glossy green head. White circular spot at base of bill.*
2. *Almost all white scapulars. Both sexes:*
3. *Large white wing-squares.*
Adult female:
4. *Resembles Barrow's. Head more triangular and forehead less steep.*

Drake.

Barrow's Goldeneye, pair, drake on the right.

Goldeneyes, pair, drake on the left.

Eider

Somateria mollissima

76

50–71 cm — Breeder — Sexes dissimilar — 6

The most common duck of Iceland. *Ad ♂* unmistakable, white above and black below. White on breast, neck and head, with black cap on crown, black flanks, belly and stern. Cap divided lengthwise by white stripe. Pale-green patches on nape. Red-tinged breast. Black wings with white front (secondary coverts). White circle at sides of vent. *First year* plumage is sooty-brown, pale breast, white line on sides (scapulars), pale areas on head and above. In *2nd year* like a mottled *ad.* In *eclipse plumage* similar to 1st year, but breast darker. Olive-green bill. *Ad ♀* is warm-brown, spotted black above and transverse barred below, finely streaked on head and neck; the only duck with such pattern. Lores extended to nostrils. Purple or blackish, dusky speculum, white borders. *Imm* much darker, dark- to sooty-brown, often with pale supercilium. Grey bill. *Both sexes* have brown eyes and greyish-green or greyish-yellow legs. — Gregarious and tame in all seasons. Large, long-headed, bulky sea-duck. Bill with long triangular profile, eyes set far back. Flat body, short tail. Flight heavy and direct, usually low; takes off with difficulty. Dives easily. Walks upright. **Vo:** ♂'s display call is a pleasant, far-carrying moaning, 'aooh-e' or 'ah-ahooo'; ♀ utters a repeated growling 'gok-gok' or 'cor-r-r'. **Hab:** Mainly marine, but a few birds breed on rivers and lakes up to 30 km from coast. **Bre:** Often in large colonies, on islands or other protected areas. Open nest is usually placed behind a stone, tussock, or some other object rising over the flat surroundings. Scrape is lined with down and some grass. Clutch is 4–6 eggs, laid early May to mid-June. **Dist:** In suitable habitat all around Iceland. Birds from E-Greenland and Spitzbergen winter and moult in Icelandic waters. **Rem:** Because of the down harvested, the Eider is

Adult male:
1. *Lores extended to nostrils (both sexes).*
2. *White above, on breast, neck and lower face.*
3. *Black cap, pale green nape.*
4. *Black belly, stern and flight feathers.*

Adult female:
Brown and black plumage, transverse-barred below. Mottled back. Dusky speculum.

Drake.

the most valuable bird species in Iceland from an economic point of view. Eider farmers jealously guard their colonies, they make protective nest sites, drive away trespassers and get rid of predators. The down harvest is now 3,100 kg (exported 1990) and total population is estimated to be c. 2–300,000 breeding pairs. **I:** Æðarfugl — Æður.

Eiders, pair, drake on the left.

Eiders, a flock in harbour, late winter.

King Eider
Somateria spectabilis

77

47–63 cm — Winter and summer visitor — Sexes dissimilar — 6

An arctic diving duck, usually found in company with Eiders. At a distance ♂ looks all dark except for white front and pale head. Pinkish-white breast, white mantle and neck, white circle on sides of vent and white forewing, forming a stripe on sides when wings are folded. Other parts of body and wings black. Two black plumes rising from back. Peculiar head and bill, large black-surrounded orange shield rising from pale-red bill, pale, blue-grey crown and nape, divided by narrow black and white lines from greenish cheeks, black V on white throat. *First year* ♂♂ similar to Eider, but darker breast and shows less white on sides (black scapulars). Head shape similar to ♀, olive-brown bill and head-shield only beginning to form. *Second year* duller than *ad*, with smaller shield. ♀ (the "Queen") is difficult to distinguish from Eider, but shape of head is different. Steep forehead, stubby grey bill, pointed extension of frontal feathering to above nostrils and well beyond lores, flat crown. White spot above eyes and an indistinct pale line dividing nape and cheeks (see ♂) and pale throat. Rusty-brown plumage, more scaly than Eider's, flanks and scapulars more crescently barred. Speculum similar to Eider duck. *Imm* darker, not as rusty. *Both sexes* have yellow to brown eyes and yellow-brown legs. — Usually found single or few together in Eider flocks or colonies. Habits much as Eider. **Vo:** Similar to Eider. **Hab:** In winter marine, in summer in Eider colonies. **Bre/Rem:** Drakes frequently paired with Eider ducks in summer and hybrid males are recorded annually. Females are rarely recorded in summer. **Dist:** As Eider, observed in all seasons and areas. **I:** Æðarkóngur.

Adult male:
1. *Orange shield on forehead.*
2. *Blue-grey crown and nape.*
3. *White line separating black upper- and underparts.*
4. *Red-tinged white breast.*

Adult female:
1. *Short, stubby bill. Pointed extension of frontal feathering to above nostrils and well beyond lores.*
2. *Crown flatter than on Eider.*
3. *Chestnut plumage, scaly colour patterns.*

Adult drake.

King Eider, male (drake).

King Eider, female (duck).

Common Scoter

Melanitta nigra 78

44–54 cm — Breeder — Sexes dissimilar — 5

Adult ♂ glossy-black, except for grey flight-feathers and duller belly. Knob on black bill, orange-yellow patch on upper mandible. *First summer* mottled black on breast, flanks and above. ♀ is dark brown, contrasting with brownish-white cheeks, throat and neck-sides. Sooty-brown crown, nape and hindneck. Whitish lower breast and belly. Barred flanks. Wing pattern similar to ♂'s. Slate-grey bill, sometimes slightly yellow on culmen. *Juv* similar to ♀, but paler. *Both sexes* have dark-brown eyes. Dull-black to brown legs, black webs. — Heavy-built, rather shy diving duck with pointed tail and round head. Whistling sound in wings. Flight is fast and wavering with rapid wing-beats producing whistling sound; generally flies low over water. Swims buoyantly, often with neck stretched and tail raised. Clumsy on land. **Vo:** Vocal on breeding grounds and when migrating, often nocturnal. ♂'s call is a mellow piping or melodious whistling 'pew', or 'cour-loo'. ♀'s mostly a hoarse growl; also utters similar notes as ♂. **Hab:** Marine, except during breeding season, then on eutrophic lakes or pools. Moults at sea. **Bre:** Nest is usually well hidden in scrubs or other vegetation in marshy terrain, made of moss, leaf and lichen, lined with down.

Adult male:
1. *Knobbed bill, black with yellow culmen.*
2. *Black plumage.*
3. *Paler flight-feathers.*
4. *Pointed tail, often raised when swimming.*

Drake.

Female:
1. *Brownish-white cheeks and neck.*
2. *Dark crown.*
3. *Pointed tail, often raised when swimming.*
4. *Mainly dark-brown, belly paler.*

Clutch is 7–10 eggs, laid mainly in June. **Dist:** The main breeding grounds are in the northern and northeastern parts, mainly Lake Mývatn. The breeding population has decreased in last decades; it is estimated to be c. 300 pairs. Few birds winter in Iceland, the majority migrate to the coasts of western Europe and winter south to the Azores. **I:** Hrafnsönd.

Common Scoter, male (drake).

Common Scoter, female (duck).

Red-breasted Merganser

Mergus serrator

Adult male:
1. *Dark-green head. Both sexes have a double neck-crest.*
2. *White neck-collar.*
3. *Buffish breast with black spots. Black breast-sides, spotted with white.*
4. *Grey flanks, dark above. White wing patch, divided by 2 narrow lines.*

51–61 cm — Breeder — Sexes dissimilar, ♂ larger and more colourful — 5

Common merganser of lakes and coasts. *Ad* ♂ in breeding plumage has glossy dark-green head with wispy crest. White neck-collar. Buffish breast with black spots. Black belt on breast sides, spotted with white. Black mantle and black and white scapulars, vermiculated grey flanks, darker lower-back, rump and tail. White inner wing with 2 thin black bars and front edge. White belly. *Young* ♂ ♂ often duller, esp. on head. In *eclipse plumage* similar to ♀, but blacker above and wing panels still obvious. ♀ is mostly grey-brown, pale-rufous head with wispy crest. Rufous neck-sides, fading into whitish throat, foreneck and greyish breast. Body and wings grey-brown, except for white, divided wingpatch, dark primaries and white belly. Long, thin red bill. Red eyes. Red legs with darker webs. All parts duller on ♀. — Usually seen in groups or pairs. Resembles divers and cormorants, with long body, thin neck and long head. Flies fast with strong wing-beats, usually low over water. An excellent diver. Walks easily. ♂ unmistakable, ♀ best distinguished from larger Goosander by browner upperparts,

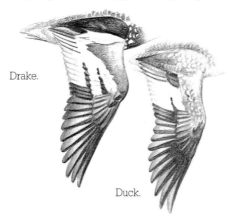

Drake.

Duck.

Female:
1. *Pale-rufous head. Indistinct division between brown head and grey body.*
2. *White wing patch, divided by narrow dark stripe.*
3. *Grey body, paler flanks.*

paler head and neck grading into breast and foreneck without sharp division of colours, less well defined chin-patch and more wispy crest. **Vo:** Usually silent except during courtship; ♂ utters a rasping 'purr' and ♀ a guttural 'karr', sometimes also heard in flight. **Hab:** In breeding season lakes, rivers and coastal areas, rarely in the Central Highlands. Winters and moults (males) on coast, rarely on freshwater in winter. Main food on freshwater are sticklebacks (*Gasterosteus aculeatus*). **Bre:** Nest is lined with dry vegetation and down, well hidden in vegetation or in hollows or crevices etc. Clutch of 8–10 eggs laid in June. **Dist:** Breeds in suitable habitats all over Iceland. Seen on all coasts in winter. Some numbers migrate to the British Isles. **I:** Toppönd.

Red-breasted Merganser, male (drake).

Red-breasted Merganser, female (duck) with young.

Goosander
Mergus merganser 80

58–66 cm — Breeder — Sexes dissimilar, ♂ larger and more colourful — 6

The largest freshwater duck in Iceland. At a distance *ad ♂* looks black above and white below. Glossy greenish-black head, with crispy nape instead of crest. Other parts mainly white, tinged with creamy-yellow below. Black back and grey stern. Large white patch on inner wing, dark front of wing and primaries. In *eclipse plumage* similar to ♀, but darker above with paler flanks. ♀ has grey body and brown head. Bright-rufous crested head and neck with white chin. Sharp contrast between neck and whitish-grey breast. Blue-grey above, paler flanks and white belly. White undivided speculum patch. *Both sexes* have red legs and long, narrow red bill with black nail, duller on ♀. Brown eyes. — Usually found in small groups. Resembles Red-breasted Merganser in habits, plumage and shape, but is larger and bulkier. ♂ is unmistakable; note large undivided wing patch in flight. Colour of ♀'s neck and breast do not grade into each other as on Red-breasted Merganser; also note more rufous head, better defined white chin, more blue-grey body and speculum mostly without black line. **Vo:** Usually silent, except during courtship. ♂ utters bell-like, croaking notes 'druu-droo', ♀ a harsh, guttural 'karrr'. **Hab:** Mainly inland, on rivers, streams and lakes rich with fish. In winter also found along sheltered coasts. **Bre:** Lays 8–12 eggs in a down-lined nest, placed in holes or crevices in cliffs or banks; also among bushes and heather or even in buildings or old Raven nests. **Dist:** Rare

Adult male:
1. Dark-green head, without crest.
2. Creamy-white body, black back.
3. Large white wing-panels, black wingtips.

Female:
1. Both sexes have red, narrow bill.
2. Drooping crest on bright-rufous head. White chin.
3. Clear contrast between rufous neck and pale breast.
4. Blue-grey body, paler belly.

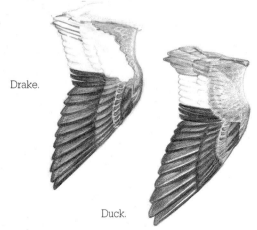

Drake.

Duck.

breeder all over Iceland, mainly in lowland areas but also in the interior. Largest wintering concentration found on Lake Mývatn. Males may migrate to N-Norway to moult. **I:** Gulönd.

Goosander, male (drake).

Goosander, female (duck).

Whooper Swan

Cygnus cygnus

81

145–160 cm — Breeder — Sexes similar — 7

Adult:
1. *Large white bird with long neck and wings.*
2. *Black bill, yellow at base*
3. *Neck held erect when swimming.*

The only native swan, Iceland's largest bird. *Ad* is all white but often stained rusty, mainly on head and down to neck. Black bill with yellow base, extending back to eyes and forwards below nostrils. Dark eyes. Black legs. *Juv/1st winter* brown-grey, pink bill with dark tip. Gets whiter in late winter; similar to *ad* in spring except for paler base of bill and some brown feathers on body. — Gregarious, usually in flocks except for breeding pairs. Colour, size and long neck unmistakable. Flight powerful, with strong, slow, whistling wing-beats. Takes off with a run. Walks easily, forages both on land and water, often up-ending when swimming. **Vo:** Vocal. Flight call a trumpeting 'whoop-whoop', also uttered on ground or water. **Hab:** Breeds at lakes, pools, fens and mires, both in highland and lowland areas. Non-breeders, moulting and migrating birds frequent eutrophic lakes and rivers, flood plains, also shallow bays and brackish lagoons grown with Eelgrass (*Zostera marina*); sometimes stage on cultivated fields. Wintering birds found in similar ice-free habitats. **Bre:** Nest is a large bulky structure made of vegetation and earth, lined with down, placed on banks, islets or marsh hummocks. Clutch is 3–6 eggs, laid late April to early June. **Dist:** Breeds in suitable habitats all over the country. Moulting and staging areas also widely distributed, but residents winter mainly in the southern and southwestern parts and at Lake Mývatn. Most of the population migrate and winter in the British Isles, mainly Scotland. **Rem:** The Whooper is totally protected, but formerly it was harvested for meat and eggs. Also flight feathers were collected during moulting season and exported for pen making. The population has increased in recent years; it is now estimated at c. 16,000 birds in autumn. Wintering birds are 1–2,000. — **Mute Swans** (*Cygnus olor*) were introduced to Reykjavík in 1958, when a pair was released on Lake Tjörnin. They bred successfully for some years and a small population developed. But later they decreased and the last bird was seen alive in 1977. **I:** Álft (svanur).

Whooper Swan, adult.

Whooper Swans, pair with young.

Slavonian Grebe

Podiceps auritus

82

31–36 cm — Breeder — Sexes identical — 4

Summer:
1. *Large glossy-black head and golden horns or brushes leading back from eyes.*
2. *Body dark above and white below.*
3. *Very short tail.*

The only grebe breeding in Iceland. *Summer* plumage looks dark at a distance. Large, glossy, black head and golden horns or brushes leading back from eyes. Chestnut neck and flanks. Black hindneck and upperparts. White lower-breast and belly. Dark upperwings with white secondaries (speculum). In *winter* dark above and white below, no horns on head. Black cap, grey spot in front of eye. Black hindneck and back, upperwings as in summer, grey flanks. Other parts whitish. *Juv* is similar. Black, stubby bill. Red eyes. Grey legs with lobed toes. — Usually seen single or in pairs, but in small flocks in spring on passage or after arrival. Short "tailless" body, often with neck erect, sharp, pointed bill. Dives and swims easily. Reluctant to take off, but when aloft flies well, with feet projecting and head held low. Easily distinguished in summer. In winter by size, shape, flat crown and angular nape. **Vo:** Mainly vocal on breeding grounds, uttering various sounds and calls, a long, descending and rattling 'hij-arrr' is most common. **Hab:** Breeds at eutrophic lakes and pools in lowland areas. Winters on coast. **Bre:** Nest is a floating platform made of rotten vegetation, usually anchored to sedge in dense sedge beds. Clutch is 4–5 eggs, laid in May and June. **Dist:** Most common in northern and north-eastern parts, but scattered in other parts of Iceland. Not found on the Vestfirðir peninsula. Most of the population migrate to NW-Europe, but few overwinter on south-west coast. **Rem:** The small population has decreased in the last 2 decades and is now maybe only half of what it was 20 years ago, c. 300 pairs. **I:** Flórgoði.

Winter:
1. *White below, on cheeks, foreneck, breast and belly.*
2. *Dark above, on crown, hindneck, back and wings.*

Slavonian Grebe, summer.

Slavonian Grebe, winter.

Great Northern Diver

Gavia immer 83

69–81 cm — Breeder — Sexes identical — 7

A large, dark waterbird. Glossy black head and neck in *summer* plumage, with vertical striped, black and white collar. Same pattern on breast-sides. Black upperparts, checkered with white, most obvious on scapulars. White breast and belly. Wings dark above and white below. Stout, black, horizontal, dagger-shaped bill. Grey-brown upperparts in *winter* plumage, with darker crown and hindneck. Whitish cheeks, throat and underparts. Greyish-white bill with darker culmen. *Juv* similar, but paler and more scaled above. Eyes dark-red. Legs brown-black. — Usually found single, in pairs or in small groups. Flies with powerful wing-beats, slightly drooping neck and feet projecting behind tail. Unable to walk, creeps on belly to and from nest. Swims and dives easily, but takes off and lands heavily. Aggressive near nest. Easily confused with Red-throated in winter, but darker, larger and bulkier, with flatter crown and more straight, pointed bill. See also Shag and Cormorant. **Vo:** Flight call a short, barking 'kwuk'. On breeding grounds long wailing cries and yodels, like "maniacal laughter", described as 'oo-ah-ho', with middle note higher. Often calls at night. **Hab:** Breeds at freshwater lakes and pools with fish, or near lakes rich with fish, from sea level up to 600 m a.s.l. Winters in coastal waters and some non-breeders stay there in summer.

Summer:
1. *Black head, horizontal bill.*
2. *Black and white-striped neck collar.*
3. *White breast and belly.*
4. *White-checkered black back.*

Winter:
1. *White below and on foreneck up to eyes.*
2. *Grey-brown above.*

In winter.

Bre: Nest is a large but shallow depression on bank of lake or islet; well trodden path from nest to water. Two eggs, laid in late May and early June. **Dist:** Breeds scattered in suitable habitats throughout the country. Residents winter on the coast, mainly in the area from Snæfellsnes in the west to Vestmannaeyjar in the south. Migrants spend winter in British Isles and along continental W-Europe. **Rem:** Iceland is the only European breeding ground of this Nearctic diver. The breeding population is estimated to be a few hundred pairs. **I:** Himbrimi.

Great Northern Diver, summer.

Great Northern Diver, winter (immature).

Red-throated Diver

Gavia stellata

84

53–59 cm — Breeder — Sexes identical — 6

Adult, summer:
1. *Bill narrow, pointed upward.*
2. *Red-brown patch on throat and foreneck.*
3. *Grey head and neck-sides.*
4. *Grey-brown upperparts.*

In *summer* with grey head and neck-sides, striped hindneck and red-brown patch on throat and foreneck. Grey-brown above. White breast, belly and underwings, barred flanks. In *winter* white on head and neck except for grey crown and hindneck. Sprinkled with white spots above. *Juv* is similar to winter birds, but browner and darker above and more extended dark on head and neck. Slender, pointed grey-black bill, paler grey in winter. Red eyes, browner on *juv*. Dark-grey legs. — Found single or in small flocks or family parties. Smaller than Great Northern Diver and bill more slender and pointed upwards. Long, narrow wings. Flies with fast wing-beats. Other habits similar to Great Northern. **Vo:** Flight call a repeated, guttural, gooselike cackle 'kwuk-kwuk', on water a high mewing wail 'eeaaooh'. Hoarse, rising and falling growling and crooning in display; pairs often duet. **Hab:** Breeds in wetlands, by pools, lakes and creeks both in lowland and highland areas, always at or near good fishing grounds. In some areas forms small, scattered colonies near coast. Coastal in winter. **Bre:** Nest placed on bank or islet. Nest is a scrape dug in soft soil with a well-worn path from nest to water. Two eggs laid from late May into June. **Dist:** Breeds in all parts of the country. Most migrate to West-Europe, but some winter on the south and southwestern coasts. **I:** Lómur.

Winter and juvenile:
White below and on neck and head.
Dark crown, hindneck and above.

In winter.

Red-throated Diver, summer.

Red-throated Diver, winter (immature).

Gallinaceous Birds

The Ptarmigan is grouped with chickens, pheasants, partridges and in particular their relatives in the grouse family, the Black Grouse and the Capercaillie, species which are very much ground birds, stout in build and mostly rather heavy in their movements, with short wings, short hooked beaks and claws on their toes. They inhabit dry regions, e.g. woodland or forest or heather-covered heaths. Many have feathers on the tarsus and even on the toes. Members of the Grouse family, to which the Icelandic Ptarmigan belongs, have bright red or yellow combs above the eyes, especially the males. These are conspicuous during the breeding season. The females of some species have smaller combs, others lacking them completely. Some of these species are domesticated, while others are hunted as game. The population size of some grouse shows cyclic fluctuations with peaks every three or four years or every ten years.

Ptarmigan
Lagopus mutus

85

C. 36 cm — Breeder — Sexes dissimilar — 4

The only wild gallinaceous bird in Iceland. The Ptarmigan moults countour feathers three times a year, but wing feathers only once. *Breeding plumage* mostly brown, ♂ flecked grey-brown, ♀ barred yellow. White *winter plumage*. Wings, belly and feathered legs white all year round. Black tail feathers. ♂♂ in winter and some ♀♀ have black lore-stripe. Red combs above eyes on males are conspicuous during courtship and can extend above crown. ♂ aquires *summer plumage* in June, a month later than ♀. In late summer the ♂ moults over to grey-brown *autumn* plumage. Young are able to fly after ten days. *Juv* (*1st year* birds) can be distinguished in the hand from *ad* by colour of primaries. The shaft is black but *juv* have more dark marks on the vane of the 2nd outmost primary than the 3rd; vice versa or both equally dark on *ad*. Short, black bill. Brown eyes, white orbital ring in summer. Feathered legs and feet, dark claws. — Found mostly in small or large flocks or family parties, except during spring. Flight fast with rapid wing-beats, often followed by glides on bowed wings, low over ground. Walks or runs easily. Territorial ♂♂ conspicuous in spring, in white nuptial plumage perching on high posts and advertising their presence, thus becoming an easy prey for predators like the Gyrfalcon. Very tame where not hunted. **Vo:** Cock's call is a hoarse long belch 'arr-orr-kakarr', hen with young utters a clucking sound. **Hab:** Breeds in heathlands, scrub and woodlands, both in lowland and highland areas. In autumn alpine areas, but as winter snow accumulates descends to lower ground, e.g. exposed slopes, woodland and even urban areas. **Bre:** Nest is well hidden among heather and scrubs. Clutch of 8-16 eggs laid late May and early June in a lined depression. **Dist:** Found in suitable habitats in all parts of the country. The highest breeding density is found in Þingeyjarsýslur, NE-Iceland and in Vestfirðir in the NW. **Rem:** The population has a 10-year cycle. Numbers of territorial males can reach 20-30 individuals per sq.km in peak years. — Greenlandic Ptarmigan (*L.m. captus*) are vagrants in Iceland. **I:** Rjúpa, fjallrjúpa.

Summer:
1. *Barred and flecked brown body, head and neck.*
2. *White belly. Feathered legs and feet.*
3. *Both sexes have red combs above eyes, but more conspicuous on male.*

Winter:
1. *Short bill. Black lore-stripe on male.*
2. *White wings during all seasons.*
3. *Black tail all year round.*

Adult.   Young.

Ptarmigans in summer, male on the right.

Ptarmigans in mid-May. The male is on the left, still almost white.

Birds of Prey and Owls

Common to all birds of prey are strong feet with sharp talons and hooked beaks. The females are larger than the males. The dignity and majesty of these birds has led to their frequent use in heraldry, for example in the coats of arms of many countries and the Icelandic civic honour, the Order of the Falcon. Many poets have likewise celebrated their power and regal qualities in verse. Some species, especially falcons, are still regarded as tributes fit for royalty in certain countries, and both chicks and eggs fetch high prices in illegal trade for this purpose. The natural populations of birds of prey have also been reduced by poison baits laid for other animals, such as foxes, and also by the widespread use of insecticides, which accumulate in the birds' bodies and render them feeble and infertile. Birds of prey have also been shot as pests or hunting trophies. Fortunately people are now becoming more aware of the irreparable damage which the eradication of this vital link in the natural chain of being would have.

Three species of true birds of prey nest in Iceland: the White-tailed Eagle and the two falcon species, the Gyrfalcon and the Merlin. They represent the largest and the smallest of the European birds of prey.

Owls constitute a separate order. Most are nocturnal and live on rodents and other small mammals. Two owl species have settled in Iceland this century: the Short-eared Owl, which nests here on a regular basis, and the Snowy Owl, which is less common and nests less regularly. Both these species are diurnal, unlike other owls.

White-tailed Eagle

Haliaeetus albicilla

86

69–91 cm — Breeder — Sexes similar, but ♀ larger — 7

The largest and rarest bird of prey in Iceland, with a wingspan of more than 2 metres. A big brown bird, *ad* scaled paler on breast and below. Pale-yellow, grey or buffish head and neck down to mantle. Wedge-shaped white tail. Huge yellow bill. Reddish-yellow eyes. Yellow legs. *Juv/imm* dark-brown, mottled buffish and rufous above and pale below, mainly on breast. Dark-grey bill and eyes. Sexually mature at 6 years, *imm* plumage variable. — Found single, in pairs or small parties (*imm*). Usually shy and peaceful, but ♀♀ defending nest can be aggressive. Unmistakable due to size and form. In flight broad, long, rectangular wings slightly decurved at end, and outermost primaries well defined. Soars frequently, rather clumsy when taking off. Often perched motionless for hours on rocks etc. Hunts from air, both over land and water. **Vo:** Usually silent, except near nest. Call is a barking 'klee-klee' or 'kra-kra', ♂ higher pitched. **Hab:** Coasts with extensive intertidal areas; also rivers and lakes rich with fish. **Bre:** Nests on islets, cliff ledges, on stacks on mountain slopes or in rough lava fields. Eggs laid in April, usually 2 (1-3). Nest is a roughly lined depression. **Dist/ Rem:** Formerly scattered all over the country, but the centre of distribution has always been in the west. Only there did it survive a drastic decline due to persecution campaign at the end of the last century. The eagle has been totally protected since 1913, but the population was still at the brink of extinction in the 1960's, with only 10 breeding pairs remaining. During the last 3 decades it has been slowly increasing; now the population is over 100 birds including c. 35 breeding pairs. **I:** Haförn.

Immature:
1. Dark, large bill.
2. Yellow legs.
3. Dark body, mottled paler, mainly underparts.
4. Long, broad wings. Slightly decurved and outermost primaries well defined.

Adult:
Pale yellow to buffish head and neck. White tail. Yellow bill.

White-tailed Eagle, adult.

White-tailed Eagle, a newly fledged young.

Gyrfalcon

Falco rusticolus

87

50–62 cm — Breeder — Sexes similar, but ♀ larger — 5

The national bird of Iceland. Plumage variable. *Ad* usually grey to dark grey-brown above, barred and spotted with white. Paler below, usually white or creamy with dark bars and spots. Head more or less streaked, sometimes with weak moustache. Barred tail. ♂ frequently paler than ♀. Grey bill, yellow cere. Dark-brown eyes. Yellow legs. *Juv* darker, often all dark and scaly above with paler feather edges below. Grey bill and cere. Grey legs. White Gyrfalcons, which are all white with dark wing-tips and bars, mainly above, are annual visitors from Greenland. — Found solitary or in pairs. The largest of the falcons with long, broad tail and wings. Flies with rather slow, powerful wing-beats, glides and soars. **Vo:** Usually silent, except near nest or during aggressive encounters. Alarm call a high, nasal yapping 'gehe-gehe...'. lower-pitched in ♀ than ♂. **Hab:** Breeds on cliffs, in river gorges, craters, rock pinnacles etc. Adults stay on territories all year long, but non-breeders travel widely and are found where food is plentiful, e.g. on coast and inland in rich Ptarmigan habitat. **Bre:** Nest is a scrape on grassy ledge or in small cave; old Raven stick nests are commonly used. Clutch of 3-4 eggs laid in April. **Dist:** Breeds scattered all over the country, highest densities in Þingeyjarsýslur, NE-Iceland. Sedentary. **Rem:** For centuries Gyrfalcons were exported annually to Copenhagen by the Danish court, for falconry at the courts of the royalties of Europe and the sultans of N-Africa. The Gyrfalcon is now strictly protected. Main prey is the Ptarmigan, and the size of the Gyrfalcon population follows fluctuations in the Ptarmigan population. Other important prey includes various species of alcids and other seabirds and waterfowl. — The population is estimated to be 300-400 breeding pairs. **I:** Fálki, valur.

Adult:
1. *Grey bill, yellow cere.*
2. *Pointed wings, broader at base.*
3. *Yellow legs.*
4. *Long, transversely barred tail.*

Note:
Dark above, paler below in all age-classes.

Gyrfalcon, adult.

Merlin

Falco columbarius

88

27–32 cm — Breeder — Sexes dissimilar, ♀ larger with brown back, ♂ smaller with blue back — 3

A small falcon of heathlands and other vegetated areas, the most common bird of prey in Iceland. *Ad ♂* slate-blue above, with darker wing tips and black tail-band. Rufous below and on nape, black streaks on breast and belly, buffish throat and thighs. Black-barred pale underwings. ♀ and *juv/1st winter* are dark brown above, whitish or buffish below with heavy dark streaks. Buffish-barred dark-brown tail. *Both sexes* have an indistinct moustache. Dark-grey bill, yellow (*ad*) or grey (*juv*) cere. Dark-brown eyes. Yellow legs. — Solitary or in pairs. Hunts on the wing, often low over ground. Agile in flight; flight direct with rapid wing-beats, rarely soars or hovers. **Vo:** Silent, except near nest. ♂ has quick high chatter 'ki-ki-ki-ki'. ♀ has a slower and more plaintive 'keep-keep'. **Hab:** Breeds mainly in lowland areas on low cliffs, in river gorges or on ground on steep slopes. Wintering birds prefer urban or coastal areas. **Bre:** Makes a shallow nest scrape in ground, often among shrubs or heather, sometimes uses old Ravens' nests. Clutch of 3-5 eggs laid in May. **Dist:** Breeds in suitable habitats in all parts of the country. Winters mainly on the British Isles and in W-Europe. Residents are widely dispersed. **Rem:** Population size is unknown, but Merlins are thought to have declined in number during the last decades. The population suffers from egg-shell thinning presumably caused by pesticides acquired on wintering grounds or from flesh of migrant prey. **I:** Smyrill.

Male:
1. *Short, grey bill, yellow cere.*
2. *Slate-blue back.*
3. *Long slate-blue tail, black band at end.*
4. *Yellow legs.*

Female and immature:
1. *Dark-brown upperparts. Dark and yellowish transverse barred tail.*
2. *Pale underparts, dark-brown longitudinal streaks.*

Merlin, adult male.

Merlin, immature.

Short-eared Owl

Asio flammeus 89

36–39 cm — Breeder — Sexes similar, but ♀ larger — 4

The only owl breeding regularly in Iceland. Buffish above,
streaked dark. Heavily streaked on throat and breast; belly paler.
Round head, pale face with dark eye marks and small ear tufts.
Long wings, pale below with dark carpal patches and tips on
both sides. Dark bars on tail. Looks pale in flight. Yellow eyes.
Short, black bill. Pale, feathered feet with black claws. —
Solitary; most commonly seen during twilight hours. Slow wing-
beats, wavering flight, often glides with wings held forward.
Easily distinguished from Snowy Owl; Long-eared Owl (*Asio
otus*), an annual winter visitor, has different carpal and wing tip
marks, longer ear tufts and is darker above with more heavily
streaked breast and belly. **Vo:** Usually silent except on breeding
grounds. Call a sneezing bark 'kee-aw'. ♂'s courtship call, a
repeated, deep 'boo-boo-boo' usually uttered during circling
display-flight. ♀ has grating 'gweek' call. Also claps wings. **Hab:**
Breeds in heath, grass or scrubland, often in wet areas. Wintering
birds mostly found in wooded areas. **Bre:** Nest on ground among
heather or brushwood. Clutch of 4-10 eggs laid in May. **Dist:**
Breeds scattered in lowland areas all around the country.
Wintering areas presumably in W-Europe; some few birds winter
in Iceland. **Rem:** A new immigrant, first breeding record from
1912. **I:** Brandugla.

1. Rounded head. Eyes on front of face.
2. Long, broad wings. Black, carpal patches.
3. Buffish plumage, streaked dark.

Snowy Owl

Nyctea scandiaca 90

53–66 cm — Annual visitor/Irregular breeder — Sexes similar, ♀
bigger and more barred — 7

Large white owl with wingspan of 150-160 cm. ♂ almost all
white, ♀ barred brown. *Imms* of *both sexes* more barred than
ads. Rounded head, broad, rounded wings. Feathered legs, dark
claws. Short, hooked blue-grey bill. Yellow eyes. — Shy, solitary
and mainly diurnal. Powerful flight, with slow glides. **Vo:** Usually
silent except on breeding grounds. ♂'s call a loud, harsh bark;
♀'s a higher pitched mew and squeal. **Hab/Dist:** Nesting
restricted to parts of the Central Highlands. Vagrants observed
in all regions and at all seasons, but most records come from the
highlands or adjacent areas. **Br:** Breeds in sparsely vegetated
lava fields or in areas grown with willow; eggs 5-10. **Rem:** Has
long been known as regular visitor from Greenland. The first
breeding record is from Ódáðahraun in the Central Highlands in
1932. In the following decades several nests were found, but
none since the mid 1970's. The main prey of this renowned
lemming predator in Iceland is birds, mainly Ptarmigan and
goslings, but also waders and passerines. **I:** Snæugla.

Male:
1. Rounded head.
2. Long, broad, rounded wings.
3. Shaggy feet, black claws.

Note:
Female more barred than adult male,
which is almost white.

Short-eared Owl.

Snowy Owl, male.

Passerines

More than 60% of the known species of birds belong to the order Passeriformes. A foot developed for perching, with three toes pointing forwards and one backwards, is one of the main characteristics of the order. They also build extremely well-made nests in which the young hatch out blind and bare. Most passerines have specially-developed muscles in their throats which make it possible for them to sing melodiously and in long rhythmical phrases. The form of the beaks differentiates groups according to their feeding habits: insect-eaters have weak beaks with tufts of hair in the corners of the mouth to enable them to catch insects, while the beaks of seed-eaters are short and strong. Nine species of passerines are regular breeders in Iceland, while a further seven have nested here without becoming permanent residents. Three commonly-sighted vagrants and also the Swift, which is actually a member of a different order, are included here, for the sake of convenience. The main reason so few passerines are found in Iceland is the absence of trees and woodland, which in turn means a limited range of insect life. Increasing afforestation has a direct influence on bird life, both in terms of the number of individuals and the variety of species.

Raven

Corvus corax

91

60–67 cm — Breeder — Sexes identical — 6

This large passerine is the only corvid breeding in Iceland. All black; *ad* glossy green or purple on head and above, *juv* browner and less glossy. Shaggy feathers on throat. Heavy bill with feathered inner part of upper mandible. Bill, eyes and legs black. — Usually seen in pairs or groups and flocks. Flight powerful with fast beats, outermost primaries hand-formed. Often dives with wings closed and performs all kinds of aerobatics, also glides and soars. Wedge-shaped tail. **Vo:** A repeated, deep 'prruk' or 'koo-rook', also a high metallic 'tok'. Alarm call a repeated 'kraa-kraa'. Many other croaking and clucking notes. **Hab:** Breeds on cliffs in vegetated areas, both in highlands and lowlands in all parts of the country. In the flat Southern Lowlands it uses deserted buildings, towers, power-masts etc. Very rarely in trees. Non-breeders concentrate in areas where food is plentiful. Breeders tend to stay on territories all year, non-breeders winter near urban areas and roost communally on cliffs. **Bre:** Nest a heavy structure made of sticks, bones, barbed wire, lined with wool, moss etc., placed on ledges or in cavities. Clutch of 4-6 eggs laid late March to mid-April. **Dist:** Everywhere in suitable habitats. Resident. **Rem:** The Raven is a bird of folklore and superstition. It is unprotected in Iceland because of alleged egg thefts from waterfowl colonies and killing of newborn lambs. Persecution varies between areas; in some districts everything is done to exterminate them, in other areas the reverse is true and Ravens even nest on barns and are fed in winter. **I:** Hrafn.

1. All black and glossy.
2. Primaries spread in flight.
3. Wedge-shaped tail.

Rook

Corvus frugilegus

92

44–47 cm — Vagrant — Sexes identical — 4

All black; *ad* glossy, mainly on head, with whitish face; nostrils, chin and lores bare. Loose thigh feathers; 'bushy trousers'. Rounded tail. *Juv* duller, with feathered face, chin and lores bare from Jan-Feb, nostrils from spring. Bill dark-grey, paler on *ad*, esp. at base. Black bill and legs. — In Iceland usually single, but sometimes small groups arrive. Flight more elegant than Raven's, with more elastic beats. Hops on ground. Sometimes with peaked crown. **Vo:** Variable vocabulary. Usual notes 'kaw' or 'kaaa'. Voice higher and more nasal than Carrion Crow's. **Hab/Dist/Rem:** Common vagrant, but numbers vary greatly between years. Observed in many kinds of habitats such as hayfields, shores, woodland and urban areas, mainly in southern parts of Iceland. Arrives October to April/May; some stay the winter. **I:** Bláhrafn.

Adult:
1. Bare face, nostrils, lores and chin.
2. Loose thigh feathers or 'trousers'.
3. Rounded tail.

Juvenile:
Nostrils, lores and chin feathered.

Raven, adult.

Rook, adult.

Hooded Crow
Corvus corone cornix   93

45–49 cm — Vagrant — Sexes identical — 5

Unmistakable black and grey crow. Black except for grey back, lower breast, belly and underwing-coverts. Square tail. Dark-grey to black bill, eyes and legs. — In Iceland mainly observed single. Flies with more deliberate wing-beats than Rook. Much greyer and larger than Jackdaw. **Vo:** A harsh, croaking 'kraa' repeated 3-4 times; also querulous, higher 'keerk' and a plaintive, metallic 'honk'. **Hab/Dist/Rem:** Found in similar habitat as Rook and Jackdaw, but less common. Arrives August to May, mainly in autumn (Sept-Nov) and spring (March-April), particularly in East and Southeast. — Carrion Crow (*C.c. corone*) has never been observed in the country. **I:** Grákráka.

1. *Grey back.*
2. *Grey belly.*
3. *Black head, neck and upperbreast, also tail and wings.*

Jackdaw
Corvus monedula   94

32–34 cm — Vagrant — Sexes identical — 4

Small and compact, pigeon-sized crow. Black or dark-grey with bluish-grey nape and sides of neck. Contrasting glossy black cap and throat. Some individuals of subspecies *C.m. monedula* have whitish collar. *Juv* almost all black-brown. Black bill and legs. Pale-grey eyes. — Sociable. Flight powerful and fast, pigeon-like, quicker and with deeper wing-beats than Hooded Crow and Raven. Rather narrow wings, slightly spread tips visible in flight. **Vo:** Short and high 'chak'; alarm call a repeated 'chaka-chaka' or 'cheek'. Also shrill 'kya' and 'keeaw'. **Hab:** Found in urban areas, forest plantations, around farms and on coast. **Br:** Has attempted breeding in Iceland. **Dist:** Rather frequent spring (March to mid-May) and autumn vagrant (September to December, peak in late October). Occurs mainly from Austfirðir in the east to Faxaflói in the west. **Rem:** Icelandic museum specimens belong to the Scandinavian subspecies *C.m. monedula* and the British and W-European subspecies *C.m. spermologus*. **I:** Dvergkráka.

Adult:
1. *Pale nape and neck-sides.*
2. *Pale-grey eyes.*
3. *Other parts dark-grey to black.*

Hooded Crow.

Jackdaw, adult (*C.m. monedula*)

Starling

Sturnus vulgaris

95

20.5–22.5 cm — Breeder — Sexes similar — 2

A compact, medium-sized, dark songbird mainly associated with urban areas. Rather long, pointed bill and flat forehead. Short, pointed, triangular wings. Short and broad tail. In *summer* black with blue, green or purple metallic sheen. Few spots, mainly above. Yellow bill. *Winter* plumage is finely spotted buff above and white below, spots are pale feather tips. Brown bill. *Juv* grey-brown with pale throat and streaks on breast and belly. Brown bill. Moults over to *ad* plumage July to October, when intermediate plumage stages often occur (see photo p. 185). All year and age classes: brown eyes and reddish legs. — Gregarious, except during breeding season; roosts in flocks in parks and on buildings. Flight direct (not undulating as thrushes) with rapid beats; often glides. Flight silhouette characteristic. Runs or walks on ground. Sings from perch with drooping wings and shaggy throat feathers. **Vo:** Call a harsh, noisy 'tcheerr' and a whistling 'tsoo-ee'. Song variable, a medley of whistles, clicking notes, rattles and chuckles, woven into a long, rambling song combined with much mimicry. Sings during all seasons. **Hab:** Towns, villages and farms. Breeds in buildings, nestboxes and, less commonly, on cliffs. **Bre:** Nest is a rough structure made of grass placed in holes under roofs, in walls, nestboxes, abandoned machines and ships etc., also in rock crevices. Clutch of 5-6 eggs laid from April onward to July. Frequently double brooded. **Dist/Rem:** Formerly an annual winter visitor and variable numbers still appear every year. Started breeding in Hornafjörður in the southeast c. 1940. Colonized Reykjavík after 1960 and has spread out from the city and is now breeding in many places in S, SW and W, scattered but slowly establishing elsewhere. **I:** Stari.

Adult:
1. Long and pointed bill, yellow in spring trough summer, dark in winter.
2. Short, acuminate wings.
3. Dark, spotted plumage. Spots fade in summer, then with metallic sheen.
4. Reddish legs.

Starling, late winter.

Starling, in autumn.

Snow Bunting
Plectrophenax nivalis

96

Male summer:
1. *Conical black bill. Yellow in winter.*
2. *Mostly white, except for black mantle, scapulars, primaries and central tail.*

Note:
Similar to female in winter.

16–17 cm — Breeder/Passage migrant — Sexes dissimilar — 1

The characteristic passerine of barren and rocky areas. ♂ in *summer* white except for black mantle and scapulars, black primaries and some other wing feathers (inner wing mostly white) and black central tail. ♂ in *winter* similar to ♀. ♀ in *summer* pale brown, whiter below; darker back and upperwings with white wingbars. Rufous smudges on head and sides of breast. Similar but duller in *winter*. *Juv* can cause confusion; greyish above, on head and breast, streaked black, least on head. Wingbars nearly invisible. Conical bill, black in summer, yellow in winter and *juv* plumages. Dark eyes. Black legs. — Found in family parties during breeding season, highly gregarious in winter. Flight fast and undulating. Perches on rocks, roof tops etc., rarely in trees. **Vo:** A loud 'tsweet', a plaintive 'teup', and 'teu'. Song high, rapid and musical 'turi-turi-turi-tetitui'. Sings during song flight and from perch. **Hab:** Variable, usually rocky areas from coast and islands to mountains and highland areas. Both inland and coastal in winter, often in large flocks in urban areas. **Bre:** Lays 4-7 eggs from late May onwards, often two broods. The nest is placed in holes and crevices in rocks, walls etc. **Dist:** Found in suitable habitats all over the country. Part of the population migrates to Scotland and some Greenlandic birds use Iceland as wintering or staging grounds. **Rem:** Breeding density is variable, 3-30 pairs/sq.km is common, but can reach up to 66 pairs/sq.km. **I:** Snjótittlingur, sólskríkja.

Female:
Grey-brown, dark upperparts.

Snow Bunting, male, late winter.

Snow Bunting, male, in summer.

Snow Bunting, female, in summer.

Redpoll

Carduelis flammea

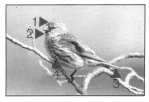

97

Adult:
1. *Red forehead.*
2. *Black chin.*
3. *Notched tail.*
4. *Grey-brown, streaked plumage.*

11.5–13 cm — Breeder/Passage migrant — Sexes similar — 1

Small, streaked, grey-brown and short-tailed finch. Red forehead and black chin patch distinctive. Some ♂♂ have pink on breast and rump, brighter colours in breeding plumage. Dark flank-stripes. Buff wing-bars. Notched tail. *Juv* acquires the red forehead in August. Conical, yellow bill with black tip. Brown eyes. Dark-brown legs. — Found in small groups outside breeding season. Flight undulating. Lively and acrobatic when feeding. **Vo:** Metallic flight call 'chee-chee-chee' or 'tiu-tiu-tiu', used as song with brief rolling trill 'serrr'. Anxiety call a hoarse 'tsooeet'. **Hab:** Birch-woods and scrubs, also in all kinds of cultivated woodland and gardens. **Bre:** Nests in trees and bushes. Nest made of dead stalks and sticks, lined with down, hair and feathers. Breeds in April-July, usually more than one brood, eggs 4-6. **Dist:** Widespread in suitable habitats. Population unstable, some years in great numbers in some areas, in other years only few found. **Rem:** The Redpoll is the only established breeding bird in Iceland that nests exclusively in trees and bushes, esp. birch. As a result of increased horticulture in this century the Redpoll is now common in many towns and also in some of the forestry stands. Icelandic Redpolls belong to the subspecies *C.f. islandica* which is similar to the Greenland subspecies *C.f. rostrata.* The latter subspecies is a passage migrant in Iceland and may possibly winter.
I: Auðnutittlingur, auðnatittlingur.

Redpoll, adult male.

Redpolls.

Brambling

Fringilla montifringilla

98

14–15 cm — Vagrant/Rare breeder — Sexes dissimilar — 1

♂ in *summer* black on head and mantle, with orange breast and throat, scapulars and forewing (shoulders). In *winter* mottled brown on head and mantle with grey marks on cheeks. ♀ browner on head and mantle than ♂ in winter, grey on cheeks and nape with paler orange breast and shoulders. *Juv* similar. Distinctive white rump and white to pale yellow wingbars on *both sexes*. Tail slightly shorter, darker and more forked than Chaffinch. Black-blue conical bill in *summer*, otherwise yellow with black tip. Brown eyes and legs. — Usually found single (♂ singing from exposed perches in trees), in family parties or small flocks (in winter). Flight erratic. **Vo:** A metallic, hard 'tsweep' and 'tchuc'; latter repeated rapidly as flight-call. Song a prolonged, monotonously repeated 'dzweea' or 'rrrrhee'. **Hab:** Found in woods, gardens, parks and forestry plantations. In winter sometimes also on shores. **Bre:** Nest is well made and camouflaged in birch or conifer. Lays 5-8 eggs from mid-May to July, sometimes two broods. **Dist/Rem:** First nest found 1978, since then has bred in all parts of the country, numbers varying between years. **I:** Fjallafinka.

Male summer:
1. *Black head and mantle.*
2. *Orange-buff shoulders.*
3. *White rump.*

Note:
Female duller, more buff, streaked head and mantle.

Male, summer.

Chaffinch

Fringilla coelebs

99

14.5–16 cm — Vagrant/Irregular breeder — Sexes dissimilar — 1

♂ in *summer* blue-grey on crown, nape and lesser coverts. Forehead black. Chestnut mantle and cheeks, pinkish underparts. Duller in *winter*. ♀ olive-brown above, greyer on cheeks, nape and below; *juv* similar. *Both sexes* have greenish rump and greenish tinge on dark flight feathers, white shoulder patch (white median coverts) and white wingbars. White tailsides. Blue-grey bill in *summer*, pale in *winter*. Brown eyes and legs. — Found single or in small parties. Flight undulating, habits and shape similar to Brambling, but markings and voice different. **Vo:** A loud, metallic and repeated 'pink', 'wheet' and 'chwit'; low 'tsip' in flight. Sings from exposed posts, a rattling, tuneful and brief song, about a dozen notes, terminating in a flourishing 'choo-ee-o'. **Hab:** Similar as Brambling. **Bre/Dist/Rem:** Common vagrant, mainly in autumn and winter. Singing ♂♂ have been recorded from spring. First found breeding in 1986, since then several nests have been found, mainly in spruce trees. **I:** Bókfinka.

Male summer:
1. *Chestnut and pinkish mantle, cheeks and underparts.*
2. *Lead-grey crown and nape.*
3. *Green rump.*
4. *White wingbars.*

Male, summer.

Brambling, male, summer.

Chaffinch, male, summer.

House Sparrow

Passer domesticus 100

14–15.5 cm — Vagrant/Rare breeder — Sexes dissimilar — 1

A compact sparrow, rare and local in Iceland. ♂ in *summer* chestnut above and on nape, streaked black on mantle and upperwings. Grey crown, black throat. Pale-grey cheeks and underparts, grey rump. White wingbars. Black bill. Duller in *winter* with brown and yellow bill. ♀ brown-grey above and pale-grey below. Dark-streaked mantle and upperwings; two pale wingbars. Darker crown and ear coverts, divided by pale supercilium. Brown and yellow bill. *Juv* similar. Dark-brown eyes. Pale-brown legs. — Gregarious at breeding sites. Flight direct and undulating. **Vo:** Shrill, monotonous, noisy chirping and twittering notes, e.g. 'chee-ip' and alarm call is 'cherrr-r-r'. **Hab:** Towns, villages and farms. **Bre:** Nests in holes in buildings. Clutch size and laying time unknown in Iceland, but 2-3 broods in season have been recorded. **Dist/Rem:** Rare vagrant. First record as well as first breeding attempt is from 1959. Has bred since and twice small populations have developed. In the village Bakkagerði in Borgarfjörður, E-Iceland, a few pairs bred 1971-1980. Since 1985 a small population has been found at the farm Hof in Öræfi, SE-Iceland. **I:** Gráspör.

Male, summer:
1. *Overall grey-brown with dark-grey crown.*
2. *Black chin and throat.*
3. *Chestnut nape.*
Female:
4. *Grey-brown and streaked above. Pale-grey below and on head.*

Pair of House Sparrows in summer, female left and male right.

House Sparrows, two males (lower) and a female (upper).

Redwing
Turdus iliacus

Adult:
1. *Pale supercilium.*
2. *Dark greyish-brown above.*
3. *Brownish-red underwing coverts and flanks.*
4. *"Two legged hops"!*

101

20–22 cm — Breeder — Sexes identical — 2

The characteristic songbird of scrub- and woodlands, as well as towns and parks. Uniform dark greyish-brown above, pale yellow or white below, heavily streaked, least on belly. Pale, broad supercilium and submoustachial stripe together with brownish-red flanks and underwing coverts distinguishing it from other thrushes. Yellow bill with dark tip and most of upper mandible. Dark-brown eyes. Pale-brown legs. — Found in flocks outside breeding season. *Juv* leaves nest before it is able to fly and is easily distinguished from *ad.* **Vo:** Flight call, a thin 'tsee-ip'; also a chattering 'chittuc'. Song a repeated phrase of 4-6 fluty notes, rising and falling, typically 'trui-trui-trui-troo-tri', followed by a weak, warbling subsong. Many local dialects. **Hab:** Breeds in all kinds of woodlands; highest densities recorded in birchwood with rich undergrowth, and urban areas. Winters mainly in towns. **Bre:** Lays 4-6 eggs from late April onwards, frequently two broods. Nest is a grass cup, built on a foundation of mud, twigs and stalks, placed in trees or on ground under shrubs, in banks or on buildings etc. **Dist:** Common in suitable habitats all over Iceland. Mostly migratory; winters in W-Europe from Ireland south to the Iberian peninsula. A few thousands are resident, mainly staying in the southwest. **Rem:** Has colonized urban areas in the wake of increased horticultural activity, nesting preferentially in conifers. — Breeding densities variable in different habitats, ranging from 15 pairs/sq.km in heathland and 80-190 in parks and plantations, up to 320-500 pairs/sq.km in birchwoods in N-Iceland. **I:** Skógarþröstur.

Fieldfare
Turdus pilaris

Adult:
1. *Grey head and rump.*
2. *Chestnut back.*
3. *Yellow chin and breast.*
4. *Long, black tail.*

102

24–27 cm — Vagrant/Irregular breeder — Sexes similar — 3

Unmistakable; head and rump grey, upperwings and back chestnut, underwings white. Long, black tail, yellow breast and white flanks, streaked black; white belly. *Juv* similar but duller. Dark-tipped, yellow bill. Dark eyes and legs. — Found single, in small groups or larger flocks. Longer tail and wings than Redwing, glides more in flight, also shyer. **Vo:** A harsh, chattering 'tchak' or 'shak' and a quiet 'seeh'. Song is a rapid mixture of squeaking, chuckling notes, frequently uttered during flight. **Hab/Bre/Dist/Rem:** See Blackbird page 202. **I:** Gráþröstur.

Redwing, adult with young.

Fieldfare, adult.

Blackbird

Turdus merula

103

24–27 cm — Vagrant/Irregular breeder — Sexes dissimilar — 3

Adult ♂ all black, wings browner in *summer*. Orange-yellow bill
and eye ring. Dark eyes and legs. Young ♂ (*1st winter*) has dark
bill, turning yellow in late winter. ♀ dark grey-brown above,
mottled paler on breast down to belly and throat usually greyish.
Dark bill, paler at base. *Juv* similar, but overall more rufous and
paler below. — Similar in size to Fieldfare. Distinguished from
Starling by longer tail, more uniform colour (♂) and thrush
habits. Mostly found single or few together. Usually skulking
except for territorial singing males in spring; they sing from
exposed perches in treetops. **Vo:** Alarm call is a screeching
chatter. A persistent 'tchink-tchik-tchik', an anxious 'tchook', a
thin 'tsee', etc. Song is a deliberate, loud and melodious
warbling with distinct 'collapse' into weak, unmusical
ending. **Hab:** Blackbird and Fieldfare are found in woodlands,
gardens, plantations as well as farmland and shores. Breeds in
trees, mainly in conifer plantations. **Bre:** Little data available for
Iceland. Both species lay from May to July, sometimes two
broods. **Dist/Rem:** Fieldfare and Blackbird are regular and
common autumn and winter visitors, found in all regions.
Fieldfare was first confirmed breeding in Iceland in 1950 in
Akureyri and has bred irregularly since. The first confirmed
breeding by Blackbird was in Reykjavík in 1985. **I:** Svartþröstur.

Adult male:
1. *Black with long tail.*
2. *Orange-yellow bill and orbital ring.*

Note:
Immature male has a dark bill.

Female:
1. *Dark-brown, mottled below.*
2. *Brown bill.*

Blackbird, adult male.

Blackbird, female.

Wheatear

Oenanthe oenanthe  104

14–15.5 cm — Breeder/Passage migrant — Sexes dissimilar — 1

This active songbird is common in rocky areas. ♂ in summer blue-grey on crown, neck and back; black wings. Black eye-stripe and white supercilia. Buff breast and white belly. In *winter* plumage (late summer) more brownish above with pale fringes on wings. ♀ duller than ♂, with less contrasting face marks. *Winter* and *juv* paler above. In *all plumages* distinguishing tail pattern, white rump and tail with black inverted "T" on end. Black bill and legs. Dark-brown eyes. — Active and restless, flies low, bobs up and down when sitting, with flirting tail and flicking wings. Usually solitary. **Vo:** A hard 'chack-chak', 'weet-chack-chack', etc. Sings both from posts or in flight, song is a brief, lark-like warbling, combining musical and wheezy, rattling notes. **Hab:** Breeds in barren rocky areas, screes, heathlands etc., mainly in lowlands. Outside breeding season found on shores, farmland and in gardens. **Bre:** Nest, a woven basket, is placed in a hole or crevice among rocks. Lays 5–7 eggs from late May onwards. **Dist:** Breeds in suitable habitats all over Iceland. Strictly migratory, winters in W-Africa. Passage migrants, breeding in Greenland, stage in Iceland in spring and autumn. **Rem:** Measured breeding density 6–13 pairs/sq.km in suitable habitats. **I:** Steindepill.

Male, summer:
1. *Black eye-stripe and white supercilia.*
2. *Blue-grey back.*
3. *White base of tail and rump.*
4. *Broad, black inverted "T" on end of tail.*

Female, summer:
1. *Grey-brown back.*
2. *Inconspicuous face marks. Duller and browner than male.*

Male.

Wheatear, male, in summer.

Wheatear, female, in summer.

Wren

Troglodytes troglodytes 105

12–13 cm — Breeder — Sexes identical — 1

Small songbird of birchwoods. Rufous-brown above, buffish below. Barred darker on wings, sides and vent with white marks on folded wings. Pale supercilia. Brown bill and eyes. Pinkish-brown legs. — Best distinguished by brown plumage, small size and constantly cocked and flicking tail. Flies short distances with whirring flight. Usually very lively but skulking, seeking food in good cover. Solitary or few together. **Vo:** A loud, hard ticking, 'tit-tit-tit', becoming a harsh churring when alarmed. Song melodious and loud, consists of rapid series of high clear notes and trills at end of each phrase. Heard singing in all seasons. **Hab:** Breeds in birchwood and scrubland, also vegetated, rough lava fields and on scree slopes. Winters along open ditches and streams; also on shores. **Bre:** Nest is a dome, made by ♂ under banks, in scrubs and trees or in rock crevices and lava holes. Lays 5–8 eggs from early May onward, often two broods. **Dist:** Scattered in lowland areas all over the country. **Rem:** Breeding density 10–57 pairs/sq.km in woodlands. Icelandic Wrens are larger and darker than Wrens in Europe. **I:** Músarrindill.

1. A tiny brownish bird.
2. Pale yellow supercilia.
3. Short cocked tail.

White Wagtail

Motacilla alba 106

17–18.5 cm — Breeder — Sexes similar — 1

Ad is pale grey on back and rump, black crown, nape, throat and breast. White forehead, sides of head, belly and tail sides. Dark wings and centre of long tail. ♂ darker than ♀ on dark parts. *Juv* grey and buff on head, with black patch on breast. Black bill and legs. Dark-brown eyes. — Constantly flicking tail and nodding head on ground. Flight undulating. Catches insects on ground or in flight. Runs quickly. Usually single, in small groups or family parties. **Vo:** Call is a lively, shrill 'tchizzik'; alarm call is an abrupt 'tchik'. Song, a twitter, embodies variants of call-notes. **Hab:** Breeds in lowlands; frequently seen around farms, in urban areas and on coast or along rivers or lakes out in the countryside. **Bre:** Nest placed in a hole in cliffs; also on buildings, bridges, in stone walls and trees. Lays 5–7 eggs in May and June. **Dist:** Breeds widely in suitable habitats. Strictly migratory; winters in W-Africa. **Rem:** Breeding density 15–45 pairs per sq.km in good habitats. **I:** Maríuerla.

Adult:
1. White forehead, cheeks and neck-sides.
2. Black crown, nape, throat and breast.
3. Pale-grey back.
4. Long tail, constantly flicked.

Wren.

White Wagtail, male.

Meadow Pipit
Anthus pratensis

14–15 cm — Breeder — Sexes identical — 1

1. *Pale supercilium.*
2. *Pale, dull wing-bars.*
3. *White outer tail-feathers.*

Note:
Olive above, pale below.

The most abundant passerine in Iceland. Olive-brown, grey-buff or brownish-yellow upperparts. Streaked black above, on breast and flanks. Paler, greyish on throat and underparts. Pale supercilium and dull wing-bars, white outer tail-feathers. *Juv* darker above and more yellow below. Dark, slender bill. Dark-brown eyes. Light flesh-brown legs, long hind-claw. — Small head, short neck and broad, stubby wings make the bird appear bulky in flight. Active, usually on ground, but also in trees and song flight is characteristic. **Vo:** A faint 'tseep', rapidly repeated when alarmed; also a louder 'tissip'. Song in song-flight or during 'parachuting' drop a thin piping, gradually increasing in tempo when the bird rises ending in a musical trill. **Hab:** Breeds in a wide range of habitats, e.g. marshland, heathland, dry grassland, scrub- and woodland, vegetated lava-fields etc., both in lowland and highland areas. Frequents marshes and shores in autumn. **Bre:** Nest is made on ground, hidden in vegetation. Clutch of 5–7 eggs laid end of May to June, sometimes two broods. **Dist:** Found in suitable habitats all over Iceland. Migratory, winters from W-France south to Morocco. **Rem:** Breeding density varies, from 5–170 pairs/sq.km,

Song flight.

depending on habitat and altitude, 30–70 pairs/sq.km is common in lowland areas. — The larger and darker Rock Pipit *Anthus petrosus* has been recorded breeding in S-Iceland for some years. **I:** Þúfutittlingur.

Meadow pipit.

Meadow pipit.

Swallow

Hirundo rustica   108

16–22 cm — Vagrant/Irregular breeder — Sexes identical — 2

Glossy, dark-blue upperparts and breast-band with metallic shine. Dark-red forehead and chin, pale-yellow belly. Long wings and tail-feathers, deep-forked tail, white tail-marks. *Juv* duller with shorter tail. Black, thin bill. Black, short legs. — Flies fast with regular beats and glides; light in flight. Perches on wires, antennas etc. **Vo:** A high 'vit-vit-vit' or 'tswit'. Alarm, a high 'tswee'. Song, a weak mixture of rapid twittering and warbling notes. **Hab/Bre/Dist:** Regular summer vagrant, seen mid-April to October, but most common in spring. Arrives under same weather conditions as House Martin and Swift. Observed in all parts of the country. Has made repeated breeding attempts, but not yet established as a regular breeder. Nest is made of mud and placed on buildings; 4–6 eggs. **I:** Landsvala.

Adult:
1. *Dark-red forehead and chin.*
2. *Metallic-blue above.*
3. *Deep-forked tail.*

House Martin

Delichon urbica   109

12–13 cm — Vagrant/Irregular breeder — Sexes identical — 1

Metallic blue-black upperparts, white underparts. White rump and less-forked tail best distinguish it from Swallow. *Juv* similar but duller. Dark bill, eyes and legs. — Habits similar to Swallow. **Vo:** A clear, hard 'tchirrip', or 'tchichirrip'; alarm, a shrill 'tseep'. Song, a weak but pleasant chirruping twitter. **Hab/Bre/Dist:** Regular summer vagrant, not as common as Swallow, seen May to October in all parts of the country, usually most numerous in May and June. Arrives under same weather conditions as Swallow and Swift. Has made a few breeding attempts. Nest is made of mud and placed on buildings; 4–5 eggs. **I:** Bæjasvala.

Adult:
1. *White below, from chin back to undertail coverts.*
2. *Blue-black above.*
3. *White rump.*
4. *Forked tail.*

Swallow.

House Martin.

Swift
Apus apus 110

1. *Black, pale chin.*
2. *Long, scythe-shaped, pointed wings.*
3. *Forked tail.*

16–17 cm — Vagrant — Sexes identical — 2

Sooty-brown, pale chin, looks all-black at distance. Forked tail. Easily distinguished from Swallow and House Martin by long, narrow, scythe-like wings. Dark bill, eyes and feathered legs. — Aerial existence unique. Flight powerful and rapid, with long shearing track, unlike swallows and martins. **Vo:** A shrill, chattering screech. **Hab/Dist:** A regular summer vagrant, found over towns, gardens, water etc. in all parts of Iceland, usually in wake of same weather conditions as Swallow and House Martin. **I:** Múrsvölungur.

Swift.

Swift.

Multilingual list of Icelandic birds

The names of the birds featured in this book, in English, Icelandic, Latin and the languages of several other countries, follows on pp. 216–224.

The Latin species names are those used in Garðarsson, Arnþór (ed): *Fuglar,* pub. Landvernd (1982). Names in other languages, with the exception of Faroese and Greenlandic, are taken from Jørgensen, Harriet E.: *Nomina Avium Europaearum,* pub. E. Munksgaard, Copenhagen (1958). Use was also made of Voous, K.H.: *List of Recent Holarctic Bird Species,* pub. British Ornithologists' Union, (1980).

The Greenlandic names are taken from Salomonsen, Finn: *Grønlands Fugle,* pub. E. Munksgaard, Copenhagen (1950) and from Salomonsen, Finn: *Fuglene på Grønland,* pub. Rhodos, Copenhagen (1967), and Salomonsen, Finn (ed): *Grønlands Fauna* pub. Gyldendal, Copenhagen (1981).

Surprisingly, the Greenlandic names for several nesting species, such as the Dunlin, were not found. In cases where no name could be found, the symbol "O" appears. If the species is a rare vagrant, the word "Vagr." appears.

For the Faroese names, use was made of Bloch, Dorete and Sørensen, Søren: *Yvirlit yvir Føroya fuglar,* pub. Føroya Skúlabókagrunnur, Tórshavn (1984).

SEABIRDS pp. 28-51

ENGLISH	LATIN	ICELANDIC	DANISH	FRENCH	FAROESE	GREENLANDIC	AMERICAN	NORWEGIAN	SWEDISH	GERMAN
1 Manx Shearwater	Puffinus puffinus	Skrofa	Almindelig skråpe	Puffin des Anglais	Skrápur	Vagr.	Manx Shearwater	Havlire	Mindre lira	Schwarzschnabel Sturmtaucher
2 Sooty Shearwater	Puffinus griseus	Gráskrofa	Sodfarvet skråpe	Puffin fuligineux	Dimmur havskrápur	Vagr.	Sooty Shearwater	Grå lire	Grålira	Dunkler Sturmtaucher
3 Leach's Petrel	Oceanodroma leucorrhoa	Sjósvala	Stor stormsvale	Pétrel cul-blanc	Havtýrðil	Vagr.	Leach's Storm Petrel	Stormsvale	Klykstjärtad stormsvala	Wellenläufer
4 Storm Petrel	Hydrobates pelagicus	Stormsvala	Lille stormsvale	Pétrel tempête	Drunnhvíti	0	British Storm Petrel	Havsvale	Stormsvala	Sturmschwalbe
5 Northern Fulmar	Fulmarus glacialis	Fýll	Mallemuk	Pétrel glacial	Náti (Havhestur)	Quaqugdluk	Northern Fulmar	Havhest	Stormfågel	Eissturmvogel
6 Gannet	Sula bassana	Súla	Sule	Fou de Bassan	Súla	Vagr.	Northern Gannet	Havsule	Havssula	Basstölpel
7 Cormorant	Phalacrocorax carbo	Dílaskarfur	Ålekrave (Storskarv)	Grand Cormoran	Hiplingur	Qqaitscq	Great Cormorant	Storskarv	Storskarv	Kormoran
8 Shag	Phalacrocorax aristotelis	Toppskarfur	Topskarv	Cormoran huppé	Skarvur	0	Shag	Toppskarv	Toppskarv	Krähenscharbe
9 Razorbill	Alca torda	Álka	Alk	Petit Pinguoin	Álka	Agpardluk	Razorbill	Alke	Tordmule	Tordalk
10 Little Auk	Alle alle	Haftyrðill	Søkonge	Mergule nain	Fulkabbi	Agpaliarssuk	Dovekie	Alkekonge	Alkekung	Krabbentaucher
11 Guillemot	Uria aalge	Langvía	Lomvie	Guillemot de Troïl	Lomvigi	Agpa siggurgtôq	Common Murre	Lomvi	Sillgrissla	Trottellumme
12 Brünnich's Guillemot	Uria lomvia	Stuttnefja	Korttnæbbet lomvie	Guillemot de Brünnich	Íslandslomvigi	Agpa	Thick-billed Murre	Polarlomvi	Spetsbergsgrissla	Dickschnabellumme
13 Black Guillemot	Cepphus grylle	Teista	Tejst	Guillemot à miroir	Teisti	Serfaq	Black Guillemot	Teiste	Tobisgrissla	Gryllteiste
14 Puffin	Fratercula arctica	Lundi	Lunde	Macareux moine	Lundi	Quilángaq	Atlantic Puffin	Lunde	Lunnefågel	Papageitaucher

WADERS pp. 52-85

	ENGLISH	LATIN	ICELANDIC	DANISH	FRENCH	FAROESE	GREENLANDIC	AMERICAN	NORWEGIAN	SWEDISH	GERMAN
15	Golden Plover	Pluvialis apricaria	Heiðlóa	Hjejle	Pluvier doré	Lógv	Ángilik	Greater Golden Plover	Heilo	Ljungpipare	Goldregenpfeifer
16	Grey Plover	Pluvialis squatarola	Grálóa	Strandhjejle	Pluvier argenté	Fjørulógv	Vagr.	Black-bellied Plover	Tundralo	Kustpipare	Kiebitzregenpfeifer
17	Ringed Plover	Charadrius hiaticula	Sandlóa	Stor præstekrave	Grand Gravelot	Svarthálsa	Tjúuk	Common Ringed Plover	Sandlo	Större strandpipare	Sandregenpfeifer
18	Oystercatcher	Haematopus ostralegus	Tjaldur	Strandskade	Huîtrier-pie	Tjaldur	Vagr.	European Oystercatcher	Tjeld	Strandskata	Austernfischer
19	Whimbrel	Numenius phaeopus	Spói	Lille regnspove	Courlis courlieu	Spógvi	Sárfárssugssuaq	Whimbrel	Småspove	Småspov	Regenbrachvogel
20	Curlew	Numenius arquata	Fjöruspói	Stor regnspove	Courlis cendré	Tangspógvi	Vagr.	Eurasian Curlew	Storspove	Storspov	Grosser Brachvogel
21	Common Snipe	Gallinago gallinago	Hrossagaukur	Dobbelt bekkasin	Bécassine des marais	Mýrisnípa	Vagr.	Common Snipe	Enkeltbekkasin	Enkelbeckasin	Bekassine
22	Jack Snipe	Lymnocryptes minimus	Dvergsnípa	Enkelt bekkasin	Bécassine sourde	Lítil mýrisnípa	0	European Jack Snipe	Kvartbekkasin	Dvärgbeckasin	Zwergschnepfe
23	Woodcock	Scolopax rusticola	Skógarsnípa	Skovsneppe	Bécasse des bois	Skógsnípa	Vagr.	Eurasian Woodcock	Rugde	Morkulla	Waldschnepfe
24	Black-tailed Godwit	Limosa limosa	Jaðrakan	Stor kobbersneppe	Barge à queue noire	Reyðspógvi	Vagr.	Black-tailed Godwit	Svarthalespove	Rödspov	Uferschnepfe
25	Bar-tailed Godwit	Limosa lapponica	Lappajaðrakan	Lille kobbersneppe	Barge rousse	Lónspógvi	0	Bar-tailed Godwit	Lappspove	Myrspov	Pfuhlschnepfe
26	Redshank	Tringa totanus	Stelkur	Rødben	Chevalier gambette	Stelkur	Vagr.	Redshank	Rødstilk	Rödbena	Rotschenkel
27	Wood Sandpiper	Tringa glareola	Flóastelkur	Tinksmed	Chevalier sylvain	Vaðstelkur	0	Wood Sandpiper	Grönnstilk	Grönbena	Bruchwasserläufer
28	Dunlin	Calidris alpina	Lóubræll	Almindelig ryle	Bécasseau variable	Fjallmurra	0	Dunlin	Myrsnipe	Kärrsnäppa	Alpenstrandläufer

ENGLISH	LATIN	ICELANDIC	DANISH	FRENCH	FAROESE	GREENLANDIC	AMERICAN	NORWEGIAN	SWEDISH	GERMAN
29 Purple Sandpiper	Calidris maritima	Sendlingur	Sortgrå ryle	Bécasseau violet	Grágrælingur	Sárfarssuk	Purple Sandpiper	Fjæreplytt	Skärsnäppa	Meerstrand-läufer
30 Sanderling	Calidris alba	Sanderla	Sandløber	Bécasseau sanderling	Sandgrælingur	Siorarsiôq	Sanderling	Sandløper	Sandlöpare	Sanderling
31 Knot	Calidris canutus	Rauðbryst-ingur	Islandsk ryle	Bécasseau maubèche	Islands-grælingur	Qajordlak	Red Knot	Polarsnipe	Kustsnäppa	Knutt
32 Turnstone	Arenaria interpres	Tildra	Stenvender	Tourne-pierre à collier	Tjaldurs-grælingur	Talivfak	Ruddy Turnstone	Steinvender	Roskarl	Steinwälzer
33 Lapwing	Vanellus vanellus	Vepja	Vibe	Vanneau huppé	Vipa	Vagr.	Northern Lapwing	Vipe	Tofsvipa	Kiebitz
34 Grey Heron	Ardea cinerea	Gráhegri	Fiskehejre	Héron cendré	Hegri	Vagr.	Gray Heron	Hegre	Häger	Fischreiher
35 Red-necked Phalarope	Phalaropus lobatus	Óðinshani	Odinshane	Phalarope à bec étroit	Helsareyði	Naulumassortoq	Red-necked Phalarope	Svömmesnipe	Smalnäbbad simsnäppa	Odinshühnchen
36 Grey Phalarope	Phalaropus fulicarius	Þórshani	Thorshane	Phalarope à bec large	Tórshani	Kajauaq	Red Phalarope	Polar-svömme-snipe	Brednäbbad simsnäppa	Thorshühnchen
37 Coot	Fulica atra	Bleshæna	Blishøne	Foulque macroule	Sjógvhøna	Vagr.	Eurasian Coot	Sothöne	Sothöna	Blässhuhn
38 Water Rail	Rallus aquaticus	Keldusvín	Vandrikse	Râle d'eau	Jarðarkona	Vagr.	Water Rail	Vannrikse	Vattenrall	Wasserralle

GULLS, TERNS AND SKUAS pp. 86-111

ENGLISH	LATIN	ICELANDIC	DANISH	FRENCH	FAROESE	GREENLANDIC	AMERICAN	NORWEGIAN	SWEDISH	GERMAN
39 Great Black-backed Gull	Larus marinus	Veiðibjalla	Svartbag	Goéland marin	Svartbakur	Naujardluk	Great Black-backed Gull	Svartbak	Havstrut	Mantelmöwe
40 Lesser Black-backed Gull	Larus fuscus	Sílamávur	Sildemåge	Goéland brun	Likka	Vagr.	Lesser Black-backed Gull	Sildemåke	Silltrut	Heringsmöwe
41 Herring Gull	Larus argentatus	Silfurmávur	Sølvmåge	Goéland argenté	Fiskimási	Vagr.	Herring Gull	Gråmåke	Grátrut	Silbermöwe
42 Common Gull	Larus canus	Stormmávur	Stormmåge	Goéland cendré	Skatumási (Válkur)	Vagr.	Mew Gull	Fiskemåke	Fiskmås	Sturmmöwe

ENGLISH	LATIN	ICELANDIC	DANISH	FRENCH	FAROESE	GREENLANDIC	AMERICAN	NORWEGIAN	SWEDISH	GERMAN
43 Black-headed Gull	Larus ridibundus	Hettumávur	Hættemåge	Mouette rieuse	Fransterna	Nasalik	Common Black-headed Gull	Hettemåke	Skrattmås	Lachmöwe
44 Kittiwake	Rissa tridactyla	Rita	Ride	Mouette tridactyle	Rita	Táteráq	Black-legged Kittiwake	Krykkje	Tretåg más	Dreizehen-möwe
45 Glaucous Gull	Larus hyperboreus	Hvítmávur	Gråmåge	Goéland bourgmestre	Valmási	Naujaruujusuaq	Glaucous Gull	Polarmåke	Vittrut	Eismöwe
46 Iceland Gull	Larus glaucoides	Bjartmávur	Hvitvinget måge	Goéland leucoptère	Lítil valmási	Naujánaq	Iceland Gull	Grönlandsmåke	Vitvingad trut	Polarmöwe
47 Ivory Gull	Pagophila eburnea	Ísmávur	Ismåge	Goéland sénateur	Ísmási	Naujavârssuk	Ivory Gull	Ismåke	Ismås	Elfenbein-möwe
48 Black Tern	Chlidonias niger	Kolþerna	Sortterne	Guifette épouvantail	Svartterna	0	Black Tern	Svartterne	Svarttärna	Trauersee-schwalbe
49 Arctic Tern	Sterna paradisaea	Kría	Havterne	Sterne arctique	Terna	Imerqutailaq	Arctic Tern	Rödnebbterne	Silvertärna	Küstensee-schwalbe
50 Arctic Skua	Stercorarius parasiticus	Kjói	Almindelig kjove	Labbe parasite	Kjógvi	Isíngaq	Parasitic Jaeger	Tyvjo	Vanlig labb	Schmarotzer-raubmöwe
51 Long-tailed Skua	Stercorarius longicaudus	Fjallkjói	Lille kjove	Labbe longicaude	Snaelldukjógvi	Papikáq	Long-tailed Jaeger	Fjelljo	Fjällabb	Kleine Raubmöwe
52 Pomarine Skua	Stercorarius pomarinus	Ískjói	Mellemkjove	Labbe pomarin	Jói	Isíngarsuaq	Pomarine Jaeger	Polarjo	Bredstjärtad labb	Mittlere Raubmöwe
53 Great Skua	Stercorarius skua	Skúmur	Storkjove	Grand Labbe	Skúgvur	Vagr.	Great Skua	Storjo	Storlabb	Grosse Raubmöwe

PIGEONS AND DOVES pp. 112-119

ENGLISH	LATIN	ICELANDIC	DANISH	FRENCH	FAROESE	GREENLANDIC	AMERICAN	NORWEGIAN	SWEDISH	GERMAN
54 Feral Pigeon (Rock Dove)	Columbia livia	Bjargdúfa	Klippedue	Pigeon biset	Bládúgva	0	Feral Pigeon (Rock Dove)	Klippduve	Klippduva	Felsentaube
55 Collared Dove	Streptopelia decaocto	Tyrkjadúfa	Tyrkerdue	Tourterelle turque	Turkadúgva	0	Collared Dove	Tyrkerdue	Turkduva	Turkentaube
56 Turtle Dove	Streptopelia turtur	Turtildúfa	Turteldue	Tourterelle des bois	Turtildúgva	0	Turtle Dove	Turteldue	Turturduva	Turteltaube

ENGLISH | LATIN | ICELANDIC | DANISH | FRENCH | FAROESE | GREENLANDIC | AMERICAN | NORWEGIAN | SWEDISH | GERMAN

WATERFOWLS AND OTHER WETLAND BIRDS pp. 120-169

ENGLISH	LATIN	ICELANDIC	DANISH	FRENCH	FAROESE	GREENLANDIC	AMERICAN	NORWEGIAN	SWEDISH	GERMAN
57 Wood Pigeon	Columba palumbus	Hringdúfa	Ringdue	Pigeon ramier	Mánadúgva	0	Wood Pigeon	Ringdue	Ringduva	Ringeltaube
58 Greylag Goose	Anser anser	Grágæs	Grågås	Oie cendrée	Grágás	0	Greylag Goose	Grågås	Grågås	Graugans
59 Pink-footed Goose	Anser brachyrhynchus	Heiðagæs	Kortnæbbet gås	Oie á bec court	Íslandsgás	Nerdleq Siggukitsoq	Pink-footed Goose	Kortnebbgås	Spetsbergsgås	Kurzschnabelganz
60 White-fronted Goose	Anser albifrons	Blesgæs	Blisgås	Oie rieuse	Korngás	Nerdleq	Greater White-fronted Goose	Tundragås	Blåsgås	Blässgans
61 Barnacle Goose	Branta leucopsis	Helsingi	Bramgås	Bernache nonnette	Brandgás	Nerdlernarnaq	Barnacle Goose	Hvitkinngås	Vitkindad gås	Weisswangengans
62 Brent Goose	Branta bernicla	Margæs	Knortegås	Bernache cravant	Helsigás	Nerdlernaq	Brant	Ringgås	Prutgås	Ringelgans
63 Mallard	Anas platyrhynchos	Stokkönd	Gråand	Canard col-vert	Vildunna	Qêrdlutôq	Mallard	Stokkand	Gräsand	Stockente
64 Teal	Anas crecca	Urtönd	Krikand	Sarcelle d'hiver	Krikkont	Qêrdlutôrnaq	Green-winged Teal	Krikkand	Kricka	Krickente
65 Wigeon	Anas penelope	Rauðhöfðaönd	Pibeand	Canard siffleur	Pipont	Vagr.	Eurasian Wigeon	Brunnakke	Bläsand	Pfeifente
66 Gadwall	Anas strepera	Gargönd	Knarand	Canard chipeau	Sutlont	Vagr.	Gadwall	Shadderand	Snatterand	Schnatterente
67 Pintail	Anas acuta	Grafönd	Spidsand	Canard pilet	Stikkont	0	Northern Pintail	Stjertand	Stjärtand	Spiessente
68 Shoveller	Anas clypeata	Skeiðönd	Skeand	Canard souchet	Spónont	0	Northern Shoveler	Skeand	Skedand	Löffelente
69 Scaup	Aythya marila	Duggönd	Bjergand	Canard milouinan	Gråboka	Vagr.	Greater Scaup	Bergand	Bergand	Bergente
70 Tufted Duck	Aythya fuligula	Skúfönd	Troldand	Canard morillon	Trøllont	Vagr.	Tufted Duck	Toppand	Vigg	Reiherente

ENGLISH	LATIN	ICELANDIC	DANISH	FRENCH	FAROESE	GREENLANDIC	AMERICAN	NORWEGIAN	SWEDISH	GERMAN
71 Pochard	Aythya ferina	Skutulönd	Taffeland	Canard miloun	Móruont	0	Common Pochard	Taffeland	Brunand	Tafelente
72 Harlequin Duck	Histrionicus histrionicus	Straumönd	Strømand	Garrot arlequin	Brimont	Tórnaviarssuk	Harlequin Duck	Harlekinand	Strömand	Kragenente
73 Long-tailed Duck	Clangula hyemalis	Hávella	Havlit	Canard de Miquelon	Øgvella	Agdleq	Oldsquaw	Havelle	Alfågel	Eisente
74 Barrow's Goldeneye	Bucephala islandica	Húsönd	Islandsk hvinand	Garrot islandais	Íslendsk hvinont	Niaqortôq	Barrow's Goldeneye	Islandsand	Islandskmipa	Spatelente
75 Goldeneye	Bucephala clangula	Hvinönd	Hvinand	Canard garrot	Hvinont	Vagr.	Common Goldeneye	Kvinand	Knipa	Schnellente
76 Eider	Somateria mollissima	Æðarfugl	Ederfugl	Eider a duvet	Æða	Miteq sujoratôq	Common Eider	Ærfugl	Eider	Eiderente
77 King Eider	Somateria spectabilis	Æðarkóngur	Kongeederfugl	Eider à tête grise	Æðukongur	Miteq sujorakitsoq	King Eider	Prakteerfugl	Praktejder	Pracht-eiderente
78 Common Scoter	Melanitta nigra	Hrafnsönd	Sortand	Macreuse noire	Kolont	Vagr.	Black Scoter	Svartand	Sjöorre	Trauerente
79 Red-breasted Merganser	Mergus serrator	Toppönd	Toppet skallesluger	Harle huppé	Toppont	Pâq	Red-breasted Merganser	Siland	Småskrake	Mittelsäger
80 Goosander	Mergus merganser	Gulönd	Stor skallesluger	Harle bièvre	Tannont	0	Common Merganser	Laksand	Storskrake	Gänsesäger
81 Whooper Swan	Cygnus cygnus	Álft	Sangsvane	Cygne sauvage	Svanur (Okn)	Qugssuk	Whooper Swan	Sangsvane	Sångsvan	Singschwan
82 Slavonian Grebe	Podiceps auritus	Flórgoði	Nordisk lappedykker	Grebe esclavon	Gjør	Vagr.	Horned Grebe	Horndykker	Svarthake-dopping	Ohrentaucher
83 Great Northern Diver	Gavia immer	Himbrimi	Islom	Plongeon imbrin	Havgás (Imbrimi)	Tûgdlik	Common Loon	Islom	Islom	Eistaucher
84 Red-throated Diver	Gavia stellata	Lómur	Rødstrubet lom	Plongeon catmarin	Lómur	Qarsâq	Red-throated Loon	Smålom	Smålom	Sterntaucher

	ENGLISH	LATIN	ICELANDIC	DANISH	FRENCH	FAROESE	GREENLANDIC	AMERICAN	NORWEGIAN	SWEDISH	GERMAN
85	Ptarmigan	Lagopus mutus	Rjúpa	Fjeldrype	Lagopède muet	Rypa	Aqissseq	Rock Ptarmigan	Fjellrype	Fjällripa	Alpenschneehuhn
86	White-tailed Eagle	Haliaeetus albicilla	Haförn	Havørn	Pygargue à queue blanche	Havørn	Nagtoralik	White-tailed Eagle	Havørn	Havsörn	Seeadler
87	Gyrfalcon	Falco rusticolus	Fálki	Jagtfalk	Faucon gerfaut	Veiðifalkur	Kigssaviarssuk	Gyrfalcon	Jaktfalk	Jaktfalk	Gerfalke
88	Merlin	Falco columbarius	Smyrill	Dværgfalk	Faucon émérillon	Smyril	Vagr.	Merlin	Dvergfalk	Stenfalk	Merlin
89	Short-eared Owl	Asio flammeus	Brandugla	Mosehornugle	Hibou brachyote	Uglubóndi	Stuttôq	Short-eared Owl	Jordugle	Jorduggla	Sumpfohreule
90	Snowy Owl	Nyctea scandiaca	Snæugla	Sneugle	Harfang des neiges	Snjógla	Ugpik	Snowy Owl	Snøugle	Fjälluggla	Schneeeule
91	Raven	Corvus corax	Hrafn	Ravn	Grand Corbeau	Ravnur	Tulugaq	Common Raven	Ravn	Korp	Kolkrabe
92	Rook	Corvus frugilegus	Bláhrafn	Råge	Corbeau freux	Felliskráka	Vagr.	Rook	Kornkråke	Råka	Saatkrähe
93	Hooded Crow	Corvus corone	Grákráka	Gråkrage	Corneille mantelée	Kráka	Vagr.	Eurasian Crow	Kråke	Grå kråka	Nebelkrähe
94	Jackdaw	Corvus monedula	Dvergkráka	Allike	Choucas des tours	Rókur	0	Eurasian Jackdaw	Kaie	Kaja	Dohle
95	Starling	Sturnus vulgaris	Stari	Stær	Étourneau sansonnet	Stari	Vagr.	European Starling	Stær	Stare	Star
96	Snow Bunting	Plectrophenax nivalis	Snjótittlingur	Snespurv	Bruant des neiges	Snjófuglur	Oqpaluarssuk	Snow Bunting	Snøspurv	Snösparv	Schneeammer

	ENGLISH	LATIN	ICELANDIC	DANISH	FRENCH	FAROESE	GREENLANDIC	AMERICAN	NORWEGIAN	SWEDISH	GERMAN
97	Common Redpoll	Carduelis flammea	Auðnu-tittlingur	Gråsisken	Sizerin flammé	Reyðkollur	Orpingmiutaq	Common Redpoll	Gråsisik	Gråsiska	Birkenzeisig
98	Brambling	Fringilla montifringilla	Fjallafinka	Kvækerfinke	Pinson d'Ardennes	Fjallafinka	0	Brambling	Björkefink	Bergfink	Bergfink
99	Chaffinch	Fringilla coelebs	Bókfinka	Bogfinke	Pinson des arbres	Bókfinka	0	Chaffinch	Bokfink	Bofink	Buchfink
100	House Sparrow	Passer domesticus	Gráspör	Gråspurv	Moineau domestique	Gráspurvur	0	House Sparrow	Gråspurv	Gråsparv	Haussperling
101	Redwing	Turdus iliacus	Skógar-þröstur	Vindrossel	Grive mauvis	Øðinshani	Vagr.	Red-winged Thrush	Rødvingetrost	Rödvinge-trast	Rotdrossel
102	Fieldfare	Turdus pilaris	Gráþröstur	Sjagger	Grive litorne	Ljómtrastur	Orpingmiu-tarssuaq	Fieldfare	Gråtrost	Snöskata	Wacholder-drossel
103	Blackbird	Turdus merula	Svartþröstur	Solsort	Merle noir	Kverkveggja	Vagr.	Blackbird	Svarttrost	Koltrast	Amsel
104	Wheatear	Oenanthe oenanthe	Steindepill	Stenpikker	Traquet-motteux	Steinstólpa	Kugsak	Northern Wheatear	Steinskvett	Stenskvätta	Stein-schmätzer
105	Wren	Troglodytes troglodytes	Músarrindill	Gærdesmutte	Troglodyte mignon	Músabróðir (Mortitlingur)	0	Winter Wren	Gjerdesmett	Gärdsmyg	Zaunkönig
106	White Wagtail	Motacilla alba	Maríuerla	Hvid vipstjert	Lavandiére grise	Erla kongsdóttir	Erqorqortôq	White Wagtail	Linerle	Sädesärla	Bachstelze
107	Meadow Pipit	Anthus pratensis	Þúfutittlingur	Engpiber	Pipit des prés	Titlingur	Kugsangnaq	Meadow Pipit	Heipiplerke	Ängspiplärka	Wiesenpieper
108	Swallow	Hirundo rustica	Landsvala	Landsvale	Hirondelle de cheminée	Svala	Vagr.	Barn Swallow	Låvesvale	Ladusvala	Rauchschwalbe
109	House Martin	Delichon urbica	Bæjasvala	Bysvale	Hirondelle de fenêtre	Lonasvala	Vagr.	House Martin	Taksvale	Hussvala	Mehlschwalbe
110	Swift	Apus apus	Múrsvölungur	Mursejler	Martinet noir	Sveimari	Vagr.	Swift	Tårnsvale	Tornsvala	Mauersegler
	ENGLISH	LATIN	ICELANDIC	DANISH	FRENCH	FAROESE	GREENLANDIC	AMERICAN	NORWEGIAN	SWEDISH	GERMAN

Icelandic Works on Birds

Aðalsteinsson, Stefán: *Fuglarnir okkar. 35 fuglategundir.* [Our birds. 35 bird species.] Colour photographs by: Eiríksson, Grétar; Ólafsson, Erling; Þórisson, G. Skarphéðinn and Jónasson, Sigurgeir. Pub. Bjallan Ltd, Reykjavík, 1985.

Bárðarson, Hjálmar R.: *Fuglar Íslands í máli og myndum* [Birds of Iceland. Pictures and text]. Pub. by the author, Reykjavík 1986.

Björnsson, Magnús: *Fuglabók Ferðafélags Íslands* [Bird book of the Touring Club of Iceland]. Árbók 1939 [Yearbook for 1939]. Reykjavík 1939.

Garðarsson, Arnþór and Einarsson, Árni (eds.): *Náttúra Mývatns* [The natural environment of Lake Mývatn]. Pub. Hið Íslenska Náttúrufræðifélag, Reykjavík 1991.

Garðarsson, Arnþór: *Íslenskir votlendisfuglar. Votlendi.* [Icelandic wetland birds. Wetland.] Rit Landverndar 4, Reykjavík, 1975.

Garðarsson, Arnþór (ed.): Agnar Ingólfsson, Árni Waag Hjálmarsson, Kjartan G. Magnússon, Kristinn Haukur Skarphéðinsson, Ólafur K. Nielsen and Ævar Petersen: *Fuglar* [Birds]. Rit Landverndar 8, Reykjavík, 1982.

Granda Enciclopedia Illustrata degli Animali. Vol. 9 part 1. Icelandic edition: *Undraveröld dýranna. Fuglar.* [The Wonderful World of Animals. Birds.] Authors of Icelandic text: Ingimarsson, Óskar and Thorarensen, Þorsteinn. Pub. Fjölvaútgáfan for Veröld, Reykjavík 1984.

Gröndal, Benedikt (1875-1905): *Nokkur tildrög um dýraríki Íslands* [Some preliminary notes on Icelandic fauna.] Pub. Örn og Örlygur, Reykjavík 1975. Pp. 27-49 refer to birds.

Guðmundsson, Finnur: "Haförninn" [The White-tailed Eagle]. Chapter in Kjaran, Birgir: *Haförninn.* Pub. Bókfellsútgáfan, Reykjavík.

Guðmundsson, Finnur: "Íslenskir fuglar" I-XV [Icelandic birds I-XV.] in *Náttúrufræðingurinn* 1951-1957 and 1971 (on the Harlequin Duck).

Hallgrímsson, Jónas: *Rit V, Íslensk dýr, annar flokkur, íslenskir fuglar* [Works, vol. V. Icelandic animals, part two: Icelandic birds]. Pp. 40-76. Pub. Ísafoldarprentsmiðja, Reykjavík 1936.

Hanzak, J.: *Stóra fuglabók Fjölva* [The Great Fjölvi Bird Book.] Translated and adapted by Sigurbjörnsson, Friðrik. Pub. Bókaútgáfan Fjölvi, Reykjavík 1971.

Kristjánsson, Lúðvík: *Íslenzkir sjávarhættir.* V. bindi. [Iceland and the sea. Vol. V.] Pp. 113-316. Pub. Bókaútgáfa Menningarsjóðs, Reykjavík 1986.

Ólafsson, Eggert and Pálsson, Bjarni: *Ferðabók* [Travel Book. Originally published in Danish in 1772.] Icelandic translation by Steindórsson, Steindór. Pub. Sigurðsson, Haraldur and Hálfdánarsson, Helgi. 1st ed. Reykjavík 1943.

Ólafsson, Guðmundur Páll: *Fuglar í náttúru Íslands* [Birds in Iceland's natural environment]. Pub. Mál og menning, Reykjavík, 1987.

Olavius, Ólafur: *Ferðabók* [Travel Book, originally pub. in Danish in 1780]. Transl. Steindórsson, Steindór. Pub. Bókfellsútgáfan, Reykjavík 1946.

Peterson, R.T., Mountfort, G. and Hollom, P.A.D.: *Fuglar Íslands og Evrópu* [Birds of Iceland and Europe]. Translated and adapted by Guðmundsson, Finnur. Pub. Almenna bókafélagið, Reykjavík 1962 (1st ed.), 1964 (2nd ed.), 1972 (3rd ed.), 1990 (4th ed.).

Sæmundsson, Bjarni: *Íslensk dýr III. Fuglarnir.* [Icelandic animals III. Birds.] Pub. Bókaverslun Sigfúsar Eymundssonar, Reykjavík 1936.

Schlenker, Hermann: *Fuglar* [Birds]. Text by Steindórsson, Steindór and Jóhannesson, Broddi. Pub. Bókaútgáfa Menningarsjóðs, Reykjavík 1965.

Sørensen, Søren and Bloch, Dorete: *Fuglar á Íslandi og öðrum eyjum Norður-Atlantshafs* [Birds of Iceland and other North Atlantic islands]. Translated and adapted by Ólafsson, Erling. Pub. Skjaldborg, Reykjavík, 1991.

Thoroddsen, Þorvaldur: *Lýsing Íslands*

[Description of Iceland]. Vol. II, pp. 493-520. Pub. Hið Íslenzka bókmenntafélag, Copenhagen. 2nd ed. 1958-60. Pub. Jón Eyþórsson and Bókaverslun Snæbjarnar Jónssonar.

Timmermann, Günter: *Die Vögel Islands* [Birds of Iceland]. Pub. Vísindafélag Íslendinga, Reykjavík 1938-49.

Periodicals Containing Articles on Icelandic Birds

Náttúrufræðingurinn (1930-). Pub. Hið íslenska náttúrufræðifélag, Reykjavík.

Bliki (1983-). Pub. Náttúrufræðistofnun Íslands [the Icelandic Museum of Natural History] in co-operation with birdwatchers and the Icelandic Society for the Protection of Birds.

Miscellaneous Materials

Paintings and Drawings

It is impossible to say when the first drawings, carvings, embroideries or other representations of birds were made in Iceland. Images of birds, including illustrations in ancient manuscripts, can be found on various objects of considerable antiquity.

In a parish description from the Westman Islands, written in 1704-1705 by the Rev. Gissur Pétursson, there are drawings by Styr Þorvaldsson of men collecting eggs from a nesting cliff, both abseiling and climbing with the aid of a safety-line held by another man. It is possible to make out the birds in the drawings and identify some auk species.

Eggert Ólafsson drew extremely detailed pictures of some of the 69 species which he wrote about in his Travel Book between 1757 and 1766.

A drawing exists from the year 1776 by the Rev. Sæmundur Hólm Magnússon (1749-1821) showing a man trapping birds with a snare, and some auks on a cliff-ledge.

The colour paintings of Icelandic birds by Benedikt Gröndal (1875) constituted a major step in opening the public's eyes to Iceland's birds. Unfortunately he had no successors in this enterprise, and Bjarni Sæmundsson had to make use of his own pencil drawings to make up for the shortage of illustrations when he published his book on birds.

It was natural that with the growing number of people studying the fine arts, some of them would be attracted by the varieties of forms, colours and patterns to be found in birds. Höskuldur Björnsson (1907-1963) drew out their characteristics

and Barbara Árnason (1911-1976) gave expression to their vitality and grace in her book illustrations.

A bird book with paintings and drawings by Jón Baldur Hlíðberg is to be published shortly. It is to be hoped that Iceland's bird heritage will continue to be a source of inspiration and challenge to Icelandic artists in the future.

Films

The earliest records of Icelandic bird life on film dates from the 1930's. Important work by foreign film-makers in this field includes that of Eric Dauderl (1937), for the German documentary film archive, Commander Dam (1939), who made a film in connection with the world fair in New York in 1939, V. J. Stank, a Czech biologist and film-maker (1952) and the U.S. film-maker O. S. Pettengill (1958), amongst others.

Important Icelandic names in photography and film-making concerning birds include Loftur Guðmundsson, Kjartan Ó. Bjarnason, Ósvaldur Knudsen, Magnús Jóhannsson, Eðvarð and Vigfús Sigurgeirsson, Friðrik Jesson, Magnús Magnússon, Søren Sørensen, Páll Steingrímsson and Ernst Kettler.

The rapid technical development in Icelandic film-making in recent years, with the emergence of professionally-trained specialists in the spheres of camera-work, sound-recording and editing, has resulted in a completely new basis for the production of quality films of all types. The increased sophistication of cameras, films, processing and printing can be seen in the quality of illustrations in books, magazines and elsewhere.

Recent films on birds in Iceland include Í

mýrinni [In the Wetlands]. 16 mm colour film, 27 min., 1980. Producer: Valdimar Leifsson. Camera: Haraldur Friðriksson.

Mývatn [Lake Mývatn]. VHS video cassette, 28 min. Film by Magnús Magnússon. Emmson Film, 1987.

Fuglabjörg [Bird Cliffs]. VHS video cassette, 44 min. Film by Magnús Magnússon. Emmson Film, 1989.

Fuglar landsins [Birds of Iceland]. 26-part series produced for Icelandic national Broadcasting Service by Magnús Magnússon and Þumall Films. Written and narrated by Dr. Arnþór Garðarsson and Dr. Ævar Petersen. Broadcast 1989–1990.

„Mit den Singschwänen nach Island" in the German television series *Tiere von der Kamera*, 16 mm colour film, 44 min. by Ernst Arendt and Hans Schweiger.

Museums and Exhibits

In addition to the Icelandic Museum of Natural History in Reykjavík, the last few decades have seen the development of several interesting museums and small collections in towns and schools around the country. Examples are the Natural History Museum in Akureyri and the museums in Borgarnes, Egilsstaðir, Húsavík, Kópavogur and the Westman Islands. Birds feature prominently in these collections, and the standard of the presentation is generally high.

Birds on Icelandic Stamps, 1959-1991

1959	Eider Duck	(Æður)
1960	Gyrfalcon	(Fálki)
1965	Ptarmigan	(Rjúpa)
1966	White-tailed Eagle	(Haförn)
1967	Great Northern Diver	(Himbrimi)
1972	Arctic Tern	(Kría)
1977	Harlequin Duck	(Straumönd)
1980	Puffin	(Lundi)
1981	Wren	(Músarrindill)
	Golden Plover	(Heiðlóa)
	Raven	(Hrafn)
1986	White Wagtail	(Maríuerla)
	Pintail	(Graförd)
	Merlin	(Smyrill)
	Razorbill	(Álka)
1987	Short-eared Owl	(Brandugla)
	Redwing	(Skógarþröstur)
	Oystercatcher	(Tjaldur)
	Mallard	(Stokkönd)
1988	Black-tailed Godwit	(Jaðrakan)
	Long-tailed Duck	(Hávella)
1989	Red-necked Phalarope	(Óðinshani)
	Snow Bunting	(Sólskríkja)
1990	Wigeon	(Rauðhöfðaönd)
	Pink-footed Goose	(Heiðagæs)
1991	Slavonian Grebe	(Flórgoði)
	Gannet	(Súla)

Photo credits

Identification photos

Other photos

Protection of Birds

In 1948, Iceland joined the International Council for the Protection of Birds, and a five-man Bird Protection Committe was appointed. An international convention on bird protection had been in force since 1902; it was revised in Vienna in 1937 and an international agreement was approved by the International Council for the Protection of Birds in Paris in 1950. The Icelandic government signed the agreement in 1956.

The first real statues on bird protection in Iceland were passed by the Althing (parliament) in 1882. The laws on total protection, partial protection and hunting were brought into line with the international agreement with the passing of a Bird Hunting and Protection Act in 1954. All the provisions regarding birds, which had up to then been spread between five separate acts and a number of decrees, were combined into a single Act, which was revised in 1966 and is still (1991) in force.

The aim of the Act was to secure protection for Iceland's birds and to establish procedures when individual species are hunted, examined or photographed. The Act encourages caution in order to preserve a natural balance between the species and also seeks to prevent birds from spoiling agricultural resources. All hunters, professional or amateur, have to observe the hunting seasons, use the legally permitted hunting weapons and seek the permission of the owner of the hunting rights. An owner of hunting rights, whether a landowner or a tenant, may prohibit hunting on the property where he resides, even in the case of a non-protected species such as the Greater Black-backed Gull or the Raven.

"Protection" refers not only to the life and freedom of the bird concerned, but also extends to the nest, eggs and chicks. It is unlawful to eat, give away or sell a protected bird which has been caught in a net, become injured so that it can be caught or died as the result of an accident. It is also unlawful to mount such birds. In the case of birds of prey, rare species or vagrants, they are to be presented to the Museum of Natural History.

It is permitted to visit nests for the purpose of watching the nest, studying the behaviour of the birds, making sound recordings and taking photographs and films, but care is to be exercised to avoid disturbance and disruption which could cause destruction or death. Visits to the nests of the White-tailed Eagle, the Gyrfalcon, the Snowy Owl or the Little Auk, not to mention recording or photography, constitute illegal activity and are punishable by fines unless permission has been granted by the Ministry of Environment.

Strict controls of this type are necessary. Those who study birds know how sensitive they are, particularly in their breeding season. Bird-watching involves travelling and often staying in the open for some time, and skill and care are needed to avoid spoiling the natural environment. Much essential information on these points is to be found in the Nature Conservation Act and the Act on Hunting and Protection of Birds.

Iceland's bird life can only be enjoyed to the full by travelling around the country. Inevitably this involves crossing farm property which is often fenced or cultivated to some extent, though some of it is uncultivated and unfenced. Those who intend to travel and indulge in bird-watching should remember Art. 11 of the Nature Conservation Act, which states that the public is permitted to cross land which is outside farm property and also to stay in these areas for legitimate purposes. Walkers are only permitted to cross property if it is uncultivated and unfenced and if their presence does not involve disruption to domestic animals or inconvenience for the rightful users of the land. If land is fenced, the permission of the owner is required to cross it or stay on it. The same applies to cultivated areas. Beaches, coastal banks and the banks of rivers and lakes are places which bird-watching enthusiasts often choose to visit. Access to these areas is permitted to walkers. Article 20 of the above-mentioned Act states that a landowner who owns land in or bordering on such areas may not erect fences or structures which could hinder access by people on foot. Therefore, when it is necessary for a landowner to extend fences to a river-bank, out into a lake or onto a beach and into the sea, he is obliged to position stiles so as not to hinder access by people on foot.

Bird species which are not protected all year round.

■ Protected ☐ Hunting season

Bird species	Aug.	Sept.	Oct.	Nov.	Dec.	Jan.	Feb.	Mar.	Apr.	May	June	July
Arctic Skua												
Great Black-b. Gull												
Lesser Black-b. Gull												
Herring Gull												
Raven												
Cormorant	■	Aug. 20th. – Mar. 15th.							■	■	■	■
Shag	■								■	■	■	■
Greylag Goose	■								■	■	■	■
Pink-footed Goose	■									■	■	■
White-fronted Goose	■									■	■	■
Barnacle Goose	■									■	■	■
Red-throated Diver	■	Sep. 1st. – Mar. 31st.							■	■	■	■
Fulmar	■									■	■	■
Gannet	■									■	■	■
Mallard	■									■	■	■
Teal	■									■	■	■
Wigeon	■								■	■	■	■
Pintail	■								■	■	■	■
Scaup	■								■	■	■	■
Tufted Duck	■								■	■	■	■
Long-tailed Duck	■								■	■	■	■
Red-br. Merganser	■								■	■	■	■
Great Skua	■								■	■	■	■
Glaucous Gull	■								■	■	■	■
Iceland Gull	■								■	■	■	■
Black-headed Gull	■								■	■	■	■
Kittiwake	■								■	■	■	■
Razorbill	■	Sep. 1st. – May 29th.								■	■	■
Guillemot	■									■	■	■
Brünnich's Guillemot	■									■	■	■
Black Guillemot	■									■	■	■
Puffin	■									■	■	■
Ptarmigan	■	■	Oct. 15th. – Dec. 22nd.		■	■	■	■	■	■	■	■

Bird Names in English and Latin

The following is an alphabetical list of the birds dealt with in the Guide. The scientific names in Latin are printed in italics, following Gruson, Edward S.: A Checklist of the Birds of the World, 1978. Two columns of numbers precede the names of the birds in the list: the first, in bold type, is the page number of the relevant description, the second is the number of the bird in the Guide and provides the key to the multilingual list on pp. 215-223.

Numbers in bold, pages in plain type.

Alca torda **9**; 40
Alle alle **10**; 42
Anas acuta **67**; 136
Anas clypeata **68**; 138
Anas crecca **64**; 130
Anas penelope **65**; 132
Anas platyrhynchos **63**; 128
Anas strepera **66**; 134
Anser albifrons **60**; 124
Anser anser **58**; 122
Anser brachyrhynchus **59**; 124
Anthus pratensis **107**; 208
Anthus petrosus 208
Apus apus **110**; 212
Ardea cinerea **34**; 80
Arenaria interpres **32**; 78
Asio flammeus **89**; 182
Asio otus 182
Auk, Little **10**; 42
Aythya ferina **71**; 144
Aythya fuligula **70**; 142
Aythya marila **69**; 140
Blackbird **103**; 202
Brambling **98**; 196
Branta bernicla **62**; 126
Branta leucopsis **61**; 126
Bucephala clangula **75**; 150
Bucephala islandica **74**; 150
Bunting, Snow **96**; 192
Calidris alba **30**; 74
Calidris alpina **28**; 70
Calidris canutus **31**; 76
Calidris maritima **29**; 72
Carduelis flammea **97**; 194
Cepphus grylle **13**; 48

Chaffinch **99**; 196
Charadrius hiaticula **17**; 56
Chlidonias niger **48**; 104
Clangula hyemalis **73**; 148
Columba livia **54**; 114
Columba palumbus **57**; 118
Coot **37**; 84
Cormorant **7**; 38
Corvus corax **91**; 186
Corvus corone **93**; 188
Corvus frugilegus **92**; 186
Corvus monedula **94**; 188
Crow, Hooded **93**; 188
    Black 188
Curlew **20**; 60
Cygnus cygnus **81**; 162
Cygnus olor 162
Delichon urbica **109**; 210
Diver, Great Northern **83**; 166
    Red-throated **84**; 168
Dove, Collared **55**; 116
    Rock 114
    Turtle **56**; 116
Duck, Harlequin **72**; 146
    Long-tailed **73**; 148
    Tufted **70**; 142
Dunlin **28**; 70
Eagle, White-tailed **86**; 176
Eider **76**; 152
    King **77**; 154
Falco columbarius **88**; 180
Falco rusticolus **87**; 178
Fieldfare **102**; 200
Fratercula arctica **14**; 50
Fringilla coelebs **99**; 196
Fringilla montifringilla **98**; 196
Fulica atra **37**; 84

Grouping in this Guide

Notes